Gifted and Sent

Published in 2009 by
New Life Publishing, Luton,
Bedfordshire LU4 9HG

© 2009 Pat Collins C.M.

British Library Cataloguing in Publication Data
A catalogue record for this book is available
from the British Library

ISBN   978 1 903623 34 3

All rights reserved. No part of this book may be reproduced,
stored in a retrieval system, or transmitted by any means,
electronic, mechanical, photocopying, recording,
or otherwise, without the prior written
permission of the publishers.

Scripture quotations are taken from the Revised Standard
Version of the Bible, copyright 1946, 1952, and 1971
by the Division of Christian Education of the
National Council of the Churches of Christ
in the U.S.A. Used by permission

Typesetting by New Life Publishing, Luton

Gifted and Sent
Pat Collins C.M.

Foreword by
Bishop Ambrose Griffiths OSB

published by
New life Publishing
Luton, Beds, UK

CONTENTS

Foreword 1

Introduction.. 5

Section One: Called
1. Called, Empowered, Gifted, & Sent 11
2. Desires and Change 21
3. Intimations of a New Springtime 25
4. Fasting from Criticism 38
5. Two Disasters: One Call to Repentance 43
6. Marriage and the Unequal Yoke 53
7. Friendship and Ecumenism 62

Section Two: Empowered
8. Baptism in the Spirit 69
9. Mary and Pentecost 88
10. Guided by the Spirit 93
11. Faith and the Word of God 98
12. Did Jesus Exercise Faith? 104
13. Rekindle your Faith 110

continued...

... contents continued

Section Three: Gifted
14. St Thomas Aquinas on the Charisms 119
15. Pope Benedict XIV on the Charisms 126
16. The Mystical Dimension of the Charisms 133
17. Healing and the Eucharist 139
18. Three Types of Discernment of Spirits 154

Section Four: Sent
19. The New Evangelisation 165
20. Praying Briefly for Others 177
21. Unity and Evangelisation 183
22. Holiness and Evangelisation 193
23. Person to Person Evangelisation 200
24. Worship as a Means of Evangelisation 209
25. Witness to Uncompromising Discipleship 218
26. Fan into a Flame the Gift you have Received .. 225

Foreword

No one could deny that the Church in England and much of Europe is in urgent need of renewal if it is not to slowly die. But ample help is at hand if only we recognise the bounteous gifts of God and are willing to answer his call. Individuals and the whole Church will come alive only when we are ready to acknowledge and repent of our sins and become serious in our pursuit of holiness. Disasters and suffering can be the direct or indirect consequence of our lack of a relationship with God and wilful disregard of the guidance of conscience and the Holy Spirit. If current suffering leads us to avoid the ultimate disaster of being found wanting at the Last Judgement it is a hidden blessing.

All holiness comes from God the Father through his Son Jesus Christ by the working of the Holy Spirit and we can all become holy if we allow and encourage the Holy Spirit to work in us. If we spend time in prayer and meditation on the Scriptures under his guidance we shall grow in appreciation and experience of the person and saving work of Jesus and thus be able to share this with others, which is a far more effective way of evangelising our culture than any amount of theory and ideas. The Catholic Charismatic Renewal, which is the only renewal movement that originated outside the Church, has always encouraged this and has been sharing and proclaiming the wonders of God's many gifts and his work in us for forty years and has changed the lives of huge numbers of people who have become very active in the Church and effective in evangelisation. Father Pat Collins has been a leader in the Renewal from its earliest days and in this book he shares with us many of his insights and his solid teaching.

Much of his teaching is enlivened by inspiring true stories of saints and holy people, both Catholic and Protestant, and by his gifted interpretation of key passages of Scripture that makes it a joy to read. He rightly emphasises the need for mutual reconciliation leading to genuine unity of mind and heart, not only between the various Christian denominations, but still more between all members of the Church of whatever rank. This is the essential basis for effective evangelisation. A major spiritual step forward for anyone is to receive Baptism with the Holy Spirit. Many people think that this is at best optional and at worst an experience to be avoided. But Jesus himself was the one who came to baptise with the Holy Spirit and its powerful effect is seen in the apostles and in many people today. It is a precious gift for everyone and we will receive it so long as we pray for it, not just with basic faith in the Churches' teaching, but with real trust in God and with expectant faith that he can and will empower us.

FOREWORD

Popes Paul VI, John Paul II and Benedict XVI have all spoken of the importance of both the institutional and the charismatic nature of the Church and have strongly supported the Charismatic Renewal and Pope John XXIII prayed for a new Pentecost. It is tragic that so many people do not appreciate the power of the Holy Spirit and regard the Renewal at best as something for those who like that sort of thing, when if only it were embraced by many bishops, priests and laity the Church would be transformed. This book will make a valuable contribution to that most desirable outcome.

+ Ambrose Griffiths OSB
Bishop Emeritus of Hexham and Newcastle

Introduction

A few years ago I gathered a number of charismatic articles I had written, mostly for *Goodnews*, and published them under the title, *He Has Anointed Me*. It was encouraging to hear that it sold quite well and proved helpful to many people. This book is of a similar kind. Once again, many of the chapters have already been published in *Goodnews*. However, a number of them have been modified since then. They have also been augmented by others, some of which have previously appeared in magazines such as *Spirituality and Doctrine and Life*. As you read you will notice that there are numerous references to the writings of recent Popes. The reason is simple. It is good to ground our thoughts and actions in the authoritative teaching of the church.

One day when I was asking myself what to call this collection, the words called, empowered, gifted, and sent popped spontaneously into my mind. Not only did it feel like a succinct summary of the book's contents, it provided me with the title *Gifted and Sent*. I have used each of the four words as headings for the book's different sections.

While the allocation of chapters may seem a bit arbitrary at times, especially in the first section, overall the divisions are intended to give the book a loose structure and theological coherence.

I got a rude awakening some time back when I bought some toiletries in a nearby Pharmacy in Detroit. The man behind the counter said, "as a senior you are entitled to 15% off." I said to myself, "I'm not a senior, and if I am, surely I don't look the part!" But, alas, I am a senior. In Michigan, you reach that point at 60. And apparently I look the part as well! But when I glance back over the years, I have a vivid sense that the four words, 'called, empowered, gifted, and sent,' describe my life and the lives of countless people I have had the good fortune to meet.

I thank God that I was called into existence in Ireland, in a good Catholic family where I discovered my vocation to be a priest. I was empowered by God on many occasions especially when I was ordained, and some time later when I was baptised in the Holy Spirit. Over the years, I have been blessed with many natural and supernatural gifts which I could never have merited or deserved. As I look back, I find that the words, called, empowered, and gifted have found expression in my sense of mission. I have a feeling of being sent to devote my energies, as a follower of Christ and St Vincent de Paul, to the New Evangelisation. For all this I feel a profound sense of gratitude to God. My only regret is that I have not always made the best use of the gifts and graces God has given me. If you think about your life,

INTRODUCTION

and needless to say the details will be different, I suspect that your fourfold template will be much the same.

I want to thank the students and especially the academic staff in Sacred Heart Major Seminary, Detroit, who have not only inspired me by their zeal they have also taught me many novel things about the New Evangelisation. I also want to thank the people of St Valentine's parish in Redford, Michigan, where I resided from 2006-8. The many friends I made there have helped me to think in practical, down-to-earth ways about evangelisation in a parish context. I also want to thank my good friend Kristina Cooper, editor of *Goodnews*; Tom Jordan O.P., editor of *Spirituality*; and Bernard Treacy, O.P., editor of *Doctrine and Life* for their advice, encouragement and co-operation over the years. Last, but not least, I want to thank Bishop Ambrose Griffiths OSB for writing the Foreword and Gerard Pomfret and his wife Toni for all their help in publishing this book.

Section One: Called

Chapter One

Called, Empowered, Gifted, and Sent

Called

Christians believe in the providential plan that God has, not only for the world and the Church, but also for each and every one of us. There are a number of dimensions to it. Firstly, our existence is not the result of some kind of absurd cosmic lottery. God has called the world, and everyone in it, out of nothingness into existence for a purpose. As the mother of the Maccabee brothers said before her martyrdom: "I do not know how you came into being from my womb. It was not I who gave you life and breath, nor I who set in order the elements in each of you. Therefore the Creator of the world, who shaped the beginning of humankind and devised the origin of all things, will in his mercy give life and breath back to you again" (2 Maccabees 7:22-23). Not only has each one of us been called into being, in baptism we have also been called into new life in the Spirit as a remedy for the negative effects of original sin. As Paul wrote: "God has saved us and called us to a holy life, not because of anything we have done, but because of his own purpose and grace" 2 Tim 1:9.

As Christians, all of us participate in two universal callings. Firstly, God calls each one of us to become holy, cf 1 Pt 1:16. As par. 39 of the *Constitution of the Church*, of the Second Vatican Council, says: "In the Church, everyone whether belonging to the hierarchy, or being cared for by it, is called to holiness, according to the saying of the Apostle: "For this is the will of God, your sanctification." Secondly, in par. 35 of the *Decree on the Missionary Activity of the Church* we read: "The whole Church is missionary, and the work of preaching the Gospel is a fundamental duty of the People of God." Pope Paul VI reiterated that point in par. 66 of the apostolic constitution *On Evangelisation in the Modern World:* "The whole Church, therefore, is called upon to evangelise, and yet within her we have different evangelising tasks to accomplish. This diversity of services in the unity of the same mission makes up the richness and beauty of evangelisation."

With those general callings in mind, all of us have to live out our own unique vocation. To begin with, there is our basic calling in life, whether married or single. Then within the context of our general life's calling, there is what could be referred to as a vocation within a vocation. For example, a lay man could feel called to marriage and some time later another call to become a lay missionary or a deacon. Furthermore, all of us are encouraged to be guided by the Spirit, cf. Gal 5:18, on a daily basis, in order to do those things which enable us to fulfil our vocation. Ultimately, all these interrelated callings are a prelude to fulfilling our ultimate calling, that of enjoying the beatific vision of God, forever in heaven.

Empowered

Jesus taught that besides having a plan for our lives, God provides for us in all our needs by empowering us to do what he wants us to do. Before he ascended into glory, Jesus promised: "But you will receive power when the Holy Spirit comes on you" Acts 1:8. Paul often spoke about this power, referring to it, variously, as God's power, Col. 1:11, and the power that raised Jesus from the dead, Eph 1:20. No wonder the Holy Spirit is referred to as "the Lord and giver of life" in the Nicean Creed. The power of God comes to us principally by receiving the sacraments, especially the Eucharist, with faith. "Faith in its deepest essence," as John Paul II explained in par. 51 of *Lord and Giver of Life* (1986), "is the openness of the human heart to the gift: to God's self-communication in the Holy Spirit". That Spirit is the key to the possibility of receiving a revelation to do with the person and purposes of God. There is a wonderful text in Jeremiah 33:3 which promises: "Call to me and I will answer you and tell you great and unsearchable things you do not know." This promise finds an echo in Isaiah 48:6-8, "From now on I will tell you of new things, of hidden things unknown to you. They are created now, and not long ago; you have not heard of them before today. So you cannot say, 'Yes, I knew of them.' You have neither heard nor understood; from of old your ear has not been open."

In Philippians 2:13, St Paul highlighted two important effects of the Spirit's activity: "God is at work within you *to will* and *to do* his good pleasure (my italics)." The divine will can be known, not just through the commandments of God and the Church; the teaching of scripture and the instructions of those who exercise legitimate authority, it can also be discerned as a result of inner inspiration. That is why St Paul prayed: "we have not stopped praying for you and asking God to fill you with the knowledge of his will through all spiritual wisdom and understanding. And we pray this in order that you may live a life worthy of the Lord and may please him in every way: bearing fruit in every good work, growing in the knowledge of God" Col 1:9-12. In Romans 12:2 Paul spoke about the conditions that need to be present in order to discern God's will." 'Do not conform any longer to the pattern of this world,' he advised, 'but be transformed by the renewing of your mind. Then you will be able to test and approve what God's will is – his good, pleasing and perfect will.' Speaking to a younger colleague, whom he had appointed to be the superior of a seminary, St Vincent de Paul said in 1656, "An important point, and one to which you should carefully devote yourself, is to establish a close union between yourself and the Lord in prayer. That is the reservoir in which you will discover the instructions you need to fulfill the duties on which you are now about to enter. When in doubt, have recourse to God and say to him: "O Lord, you are the Father of light, teach me what I ought to do in this circumstance."

Not only does the Lord reveal the divine will to us, e.g. by means of the voice of conscience or inner promptings associated with consolation of spirit, we are also empowered to carry it out, even if it seems to be beyond our merely natural capacities. St. Paul was very aware of this fact. In 2 Corinthians 12:9 he recounted words that were spoken to him by the Lord: "My grace is sufficient for you, for my power is made perfect in weakness." In Philippians 4:13 Paul testified, "I can do everything through him who gives me strength." He gave an example of what he had in mind when he wrote in 1 Corinthians 10:13, "God is faithful; he will not let you be tempted beyond what you can bear. But when you are tempted, he will also provide a way out so that you can stand up under it." As members of A.A. and other twelve step groups know only too well, these promises only come to fruition if the person is humble, truly wants to do God's will, and trusts without reservation in the power of God at work in and through his or her vulnerability.

Gifted

Not only does the Lord empower us by grace to carry out the divine will in accord with our vocation, God gives us the natural and supernatural gifts we need to do so. Arguably one of the most important speeches at the Second Vatican Council was one that was delivered by Cardinal Suenens, of Malines, in Belgium. During the debate on the Church, he gave a memorable talk on, 'The Charismatic Dimension of the Church.' In it he spoke about the giftedness of the members of the Church whether clerical or lay. He wanted to get away from the idea that all grace comes solely through sacraments and clerical ministry. He argued, that in virtue of their baptism, the laity receive ordinary and extraordinary graces which equip them to build up the Church. At one point in his speech he said: "Thus to St Paul the Church of the living Christ does not appear as some kind of administrative organization, but as a living web of gifts, of charisms, of ministries. The Spirit is given to every individual Christian, the Spirit who gives his gifts, his charisms to each and every one… Each and every Christian, whether lettered or unlettered has his charism in his daily life, but as St Paul says, "All of these must aim at one thing; to build up the Church" 1 Cor 14:26.

The Cardinal's views were incorporated in the conciliar *Constitution on the Church*. God's empowering grace can also come to us in many ways. For example, in par. 12 we read: "It is not only through the sacraments and the ministries of the Church that the Holy Spirit sanctifies and leads the people of God and enriches it with virtues, but, "allotting his gifts to everyone according as He wills, He distributes special graces among the faithful of every rank." The constitution also stated that lay people have a right and a duty, stemming from their baptism, to exercise their gifts for the good of others. These teachings were succinctly expressed in par. 24 of *The Decree of the Role and Apostolate of the Laity:* "In referring to the apostolate of the lay faithful the Second Vatican Council writes: "For the exercise of the apostolate the Holy Spirit who sanctifies the People of God through the ministry and the sacraments gives the faithful special gifts as well, cf. 1 Cor 12:7, 'allotting them to each one as he wills', cf. 1 Cor 12:11, so that each might place 'at the service of others the grace received' and become 'good stewards of God's varied grace', 1 Pt 4:10, and build up thereby the whole body in charity, cf. Eph 4:16." By a logic which looks to the divine source of this giving, as the Council recalls, the gifts of the Spirit demand that those who have received them exercise them for the growth of the whole Church."

Finally, there is a Catholic belief which is referred to by St Thomas Aquinas, which states: "the grace of God does not replace nature, but fulfils it." Let's look at a practical example. If a woman felt called to be a lay catechist in her diocese, not only would she need to be naturally intelligent, well educated, familiar with Christian theology, and articulate, she would also need supernatural gifts such as wisdom and knowledge, cf. Is 11:2 , in order to carry out her catechetical vocation in an effective way.

Sent

As was mentioned already, there are two universal callings, the call to holiness and the call to evangelise. It seems fairly obvious that they are interrelated. Surely, effective evangelisation is only possible to the extent that the evangelisers are holy. For more on this point see Chapter 22 below. Sadly, in these islands we have witnessed a silent apostasy over the years as millions of people have drifted away from their Christian heritage. In the year 2000 Pope Benedict, then Cardinal Ratzinger, gave a talk to catechists in Rome on the subject of the New Evangelisation. He said that it sought to bring the message of Christ to the un-churched and unbelievers. Talking about the nature of evangelisation he stated: "Human life cannot be realised by itself. Our life is an open question, an incomplete project, still to be brought to fruition and realized. Each man's fundamental question is: how will this be realised – i.e. to become a fulfilled man? How does one learn the art of living? Which is the path towards happiness? *To evangelise means: to show this path – to teach the art of living* (my italics). At the beginning of His public life Jesus said: "I have come to evangelise the poor, Lk 4:18; this means: I have the response to your fundamental question; I will show you the path of life, the path towards happiness – rather: I am that path." The Christian message is not new, of course, but it will need to be expressed in new ways that will relate it to the people of the 21st century. The chapters in section four deal with some aspects of this challenge.

Pope Benedict warned, however, that the evangelisers will need to have patience. "New evangelisation," he said, "cannot mean: immediately attracting the large masses that have distanced themselves from the Church by using new and more refined methods. No – this is not what new evangelisation promises." The Holy Father went on to add these sobering words: "An old proverb says: "Success is not one of the names of God". New evangelisation must surrender to the mystery of the grain of mustard seed and not be so pretentious as to believe that it will immediately produce a large tree. We either live too much in the security of the already existing large tree (i.e. of the world wide Church) or in the impatience of having a greater, more vital tree – instead we must accept the mystery that the Church is at the same time a large tree and a very small grain. In the history of salvation it is always Good Friday and Easter Sunday at the same time." I'm reminded in this context of a saying of Blessed Teresa of Calcutta, "I do not pray for success, I ask for faithfulness." While agreeing that faithfulness is more important than success, surely, as chapter three suggests, it is possible that God, by a sovereign act of his Spirit, could bring about mass revival. Remember how St Peter converted 3,000 people on Pentecost Sunday.

Conclusion

In English the Eucharist, which is the fount and apex of the whole Christian life, is referred to as the Mass. The word is derived from the Latin, *missus*, which is the present participle of *mittere* meaning 'to send.' So at the end of each Mass, the faithful are sent in peace to "love and serve the Lord." They do this by living out, in their day-to-day lives, the mystery of Christ's sacrificial love which they have just celebrated in a real but sacramental way. As *The Decree on the Life of Priests,* states in par. 6: "No Christian community... can be built up unless it has its basis and centre in the celebration of the most Holy Eucharist. Here, therefore, all education in the spirit of community must originate. If this celebration is to be sincere and thorough, it must lead to various works of charity and mutual help, as well as to missionary activity and to the different forms of Christian witness."

Chapter Two

Desires and Change

You know the large, two litre, bottles of lemonade. At first, they are sparkling and refreshing to drink. But once they are half empty, they lose their fizz and become rather flat and unpalatable. I suspect that your Christian life may be much the same. When you experienced your spiritual awakening you were full of enthusiasm for the things of the Spirit. But as the years have passed, you may have lost your first fervour. Perhaps, some complacency, carelessness and compromise have crept in. It can happen in these inter-related ways:

1. For one reason or another, such as excessive extroversion and a lack of self-awareness, you may have lost touch with your spiritual desires.
2. You may have either dropped some of your spiritual practices, e.g. going to the sacrament of reconciliation or praying in tongues, or do so less often and with less

sincerity and conviction.

3. Having lost touch with your deeper spiritual desires, you may have tended to replace them with questionable desires, e.g. for things such as pleasure, popularity, and power, typically in the form of material things and influence. As a result you may be knowingly tolerating some sinful attachment or practice in your life.

If you have become tepid in this way, it's worth reminding yourself that the Lord said: "I know your deeds, that you are neither cold nor hot. I wish you were either one or the other! So, because you are lukewarm -- neither hot nor cold -- I am about to spit you out of my mouth" Rev 3:15-16.

Remember your spiritual awakening

How can you stop disappointing the Lord in this manner? When I was thinking and praying about this question, two related texts came to mind. The first says: "Stand at the crossroads and look; ask for the ancient paths, ask where the good way is, and walk in it", Jer 6:16. In the second the Lord says: "I hold this against you: You have forsaken your first love. Remember the height from which you have fallen! Repent and do the things you did at first", Rev 2:4-5. You will notice that both verses encourage you to recall the passionate desires that first led you to form a deep personal relationship with Christ and to be guided by his Holy Spirit.

God prompted desires

Those longings were, and still are very important because there will be no blessing or renewal in your spiritual life without them. The stronger and deeper the desire the greater the subsequent blessings will be. So it is important that you recall the intensity of the longings that led to your new life in Christ. St. Paul stated: "God's gifts and call are irrevocable", Rm 11:29. All of us receive a call and associated graces from God. No matter how far we wander from the straight and narrow, where Christian faith and morals are concerned, the Lord will never revoke our call or withdraw its empowering graces. If, and when, we come to our senses and return to the Lord, we will be blessed as if we had never strayed.

I have great admiration for the late Kathryn Kuhlman (1908-1976). As a young Protestant she experienced a vocation to become an evangelist. As she obeyed the call she found that she had been richly blessed with a remarkable gift of healing. Some years later, despite her own misgivings, and the entreaties of friends, she married a man who had abandoned his wife and two children. Not surprisingly, her ministry went into decline. Years later she acknowledged that she was living a lie. She said: "I had come to the place in my life where I was ready to give up everything - even my husband - and die. I said it out loud, 'Dear Jesus, I surrender all. I give it all to you'." When she returned to ministry, she was more successful than ever and went on to become one of the greatest healers of the 20th century.

matter how far you may have wandered from the straight and narrow, God will never revoke your call or withdraw its empowering graces. If, and when, you turn back to the Lord with all your heart, not only will you be blessed, as if you had never strayed, new graces will be poured out upon you. Furthermore, you need to ask yourself, "what grace do I really want right now?" When you can answer that question, you will be in touch with the action of God's grace within you. As Paul assures us, "God and Father of our Lord Jesus Christ, has blessed us in the heavenly realms with every spiritual blessing in Christ." Eph 1:3-4, and "He who did not spare his own Son, but gave him up for us all - how will he not also, along with him, graciously give us all things?" Rom 8:32-33.

One thing leads to another

Once your Spirit-prompted desire for deeper relationship with the Lord has been satisfied, you will also be motivated to renew your commitment to your spiritual practices. As a result you are more likely, not only to spend more time in daily prayer, but to do so in a disciplined, focused way. As your sense of relationship with God and the divine increase, you will tend to turn away from those worldly and inappropriate desires and attachments that grieve the Holy Spirit. You will do this, not as a matter of cheerless duty, but as a result of heartfelt conviction. So if you want to put the spiritual fizz back into your life, the question you would do well to answer is the one that the Lord addressed to two young men: "Turning around, Jesus saw them following and asked, 'What do you want?'", Jn 1:38.

Chapter Three

Intimations of a New Springtime

Early and late rains in scripture

It may surprise you to find that this chapter begins with a verse about the weather in the Holy Land. In Deuteronomy 11:14-15 we read the following divine promise, "then I will send rain on your land in its season, both autumn and spring rains, so that you may gather in your grain, new wine and oil." This undertaking consoled the Jewish people because there was a severe lack of water in Israel. God has fulfilled the promise right down to the present day. As we read in Joel 2:23-24: "Be glad, O people of Zion, rejoice in the Lord your God, for he has given you the autumn rains of righteousness. He sends you abundant showers, both autumn and spring rains, as before. The threshing floors will be filled with grain; the vats will overflow with new wine and oil." Ironically the crops were planted in the rainy autumn season between September 15 and November 15. The Israelites called this *yarah*, or the former rain. The crops matured in the rainy Spring season between March 15 and May 15. The Israelites called this *malqosh*, or the latter rain. When the crops ripened they were harvested. With the completion of this task a thanksgiving festival was celebrated. In Greek it was known as Pentecost.

The early and late rains are also mentioned in the New Testament. In James 5:7 we read: "Be patient, then, brothers, until the Lord's coming. See how the farmer waits for the land to yield its valuable crop and how patient he is for the autumn and spring rains." Over the centuries the notion of the two rains has been understood in a symbolic way to refer to two interrelated anointings of the Spirit which precede the harvesting of a great number of souls for God. It is quite possible that Jesus had this in mind when he said: "The harvest is plentiful, but the workers are few. Ask the Lord of the harvest, therefore, to send out workers into his harvest field", Lk 10:2.

In the Bible it is clear that the physical fact of the early and late rains was given a spiritual interpretation of a symbolic kind. There is an example in the Acts of the Apostles. In Acts 2:1-41 we read about the first rain of blessing which enabled the seed of Christianity to take root and to grow. When the early Church was being persecuted we read in Acts 4:23-31 about a second rain of blessing. Peter and John had been interrogated and imprisoned because of their witness to Jesus. When they were released they went to the Christian community and told them what had happened. When the disciples of the Lord heard about the opposition they were facing from the Jews and Romans they prayed fervently to God: "Now, Lord, consider their threats and enable your servants to speak your word with great boldness. Stretch out your hand to heal and perform miraculous signs and wonders through the name of your holy servant Jesus." After they prayed, the place where they were meeting was shaken. And they were all filled with the Holy Spirit and spoke the word of God boldly." What is striking is the fact that the disciples did not ask for a new outpouring of the Spirit. Instead they yearned to carry out the great commission to evangelise, cf. Mt 6:33. As they ardently desired to do this, the second rain fell upon them when the Holy Spirit was poured upon them anew.

In contemporary Christianity there are two main ways of interpreting the two rains. Firstly, many Pentecostals believe that the first and second rains refer to two stages of history. The first began on Pentecost Sunday. They maintain that the second began with the advent of the Pentecostal and charismatic movements in the twentieth century. This latter rain has inaugurated the run-in to the second coming before which there will be a final conflict between good and evil together with mass apostasy, cf. 2 Tim 3:1-5; Rev 19:20; 1 Jn 2:18-19; 4:3; 2 Jn:7. Arguably, controversial seers Vassula Ryden, and Fr. Stephano Gobbi take a somewhat similar view.

The second way of interpreting the two rains is to see them as a recurring pattern in Church history. For instance, I have heard one Catholic speaker suggest, a little arbitrarily perhaps, that Our Lady's apparition at Fatima in 1917 could be seen as an instance of the early rain. He noted that it was significant that preceding the final apparition there was a mighty downpour of rain which was followed by the miracle of the sun when it seemed to come close to the earth. He went on to maintain that the latter rain fell some fifty years later in 1967 with the beginning of the Catholic Charismatic Movement. In this chapter the notion of the recurring pattern will predominate.

The first shower of the early rain
At the outset I want to suggest that during the twentieth century we experienced an early rain of blessing in the form of three interrelated showers of revival, firstly, the Pentecostal Movement, secondly the Charismatic Movements, and thirdly, the Signs and Wonders Movement. As you know the first shower of the early rain came in the form of the Pentecostal revival which took place in Azuza Street in 1906 when a group of poorer people from diverse backgrounds and races were baptised in the Holy Spirit and exercised the gifts of the Spirit which are mentioned in 1 Corinthians 12:8-10. When they were rejected by the mainline Churches, they formed their own churches and spread out across the world to bring the Pentecostal message to others.

The second shower of the early rain
Smith Wigglesworth, an Englishman, was one of the first

Pentecostals. He was baptised in the Holy Spirit in 1907. In 1937 he visited South Africa as a guest of the Apostolic Faith Mission in Johannesburg. David Du Plessis was its general secretary at the time. Later, Du Plessis explained how one morning, Wigglesworth walked, unannounced, into his office. He pushed him against the wall and declared:

> "You have been in Jerusalem long enough... I will send you to the uttermost parts of the earth... You will bring the message of Pentecost to all churches... You will travel more than most evangelists do... God is going to revive the churches in the last days and through them turn the world upside down... even the Pentecostal movement will become a mere joke compared with the revival which God will bring through the churches."

After a pause Wigglesworth continued,

> "Then the Lord said to me that I am warning you that He is going to use you in this movement... All He requires of you is that you be humble and faithful. You will live to see this word fulfilled."

He concluded by saying that this prophecy about the second shower, would not be fulfilled until after his death. In the event, Wigglesworth died in 1947.

Over the next few years Du Plessis became increasingly influential in Protestant and later in Catholic circles. For example, in his book *Simple and Profound* he has explained how, at a gathering in St. Andrews in Scotland in 1951, he met Professor Bernard Leaming, a Jesuit priest from Oxford. He asked for prayer for baptism in the Holy Spirit. This marked the start of Du Plessis' ministry to Roman Catholics. When the Second Vatican Council started soon afterwards, Du Plessis was invited to attend. No doubt he was delighted when par. 12 of the *Constitution of the Church* referred to the charisms mentioned in 1 Corinthians 12:8-10. As we know, the Catholic Charismatic Renewal came into existence as a result of the Duquesne Retreat in 1967, when the Spirit and the charisms were poured out in abundance on Catholics, firstly in the U.S., and later around the world. By the year 2000 there were well over a 100 million Catholic and post-charismatics.

The third shower of the early rain

In more recent years a third shower of revival occurred when people like John Wimber and Peter Wagner initiated what is known as the Signs and Wonders Movement. Their views about evangelisation were influenced by the remarkable ministries of Smith Wigglesworth in Britain, and Kathryn Kuhlman in the United States. In 1981 Wimber delivered a lecture at Fuller Theological Seminary entitled, *Signs, Wonders and Church Growth*. Then, from 1982 to 1985 he taught a very popular course at the seminary, entitled *The Miraculous and Church Growth*. He also lectured abroad, e.g. in Britain and Ireland. In 1986 his Fuller lecture notes were edited by Kevin Springer and published with the title, *Power Evangelism*. John Wimber died in 1997. It could be argued that controversial evangelist Todd Bentley, author of *The Reality of the Supernatural World*, who was associated for a brief time with the 2008 Lakeland revival in Florida, is Wimber's successor in so far as he advocates a form of evangelism which is associated with signs and wonders.

Prophecies about the later rains

I have already adverted to the fact that Smith Wigglesworth seems to have accurately prophesied the advent of the Catholic and Protestant Charismatic movements. It is said that shortly before his death he made another prescient prophecy. It is well worth recounting. Not only did he foretell the rise of the Charismatic Renewal with its emphasis on the Spirit and the rise of house churches with their emphasis on the word of God, he also predicted that when both seemed to be waning:

> "There will be evidence in the churches of something that has not been seen before: a coming together of those with an emphasis on the word and those with an emphasis on the Spirit. When the word and the Spirit come together, there will be the biggest move of the Holy Spirit that the nations, and indeed the world, have ever seen. It will mark the beginning of a revival that will eclipse …the revivals of former years."

Surely, Wigglesworth was referring to a second rain, similar to the second Pentecost referred to in Acts 4:23-31. May I say, in passing, that this prophecy found an echo in a prophecy which was uttered by Ralph Martin in St Peter's Basilica in Rome in 1975, when he said:

> "A time of darkness is coming upon the world, but a time of glory is coming for my Church, a time of glory is coming for my people. I will pour out on you all the gifts of my Spirit. I will prepare you for spiritual combat; I will prepare you for a time of evangelism the world has never seen."

On the 7th February 2003, a Church of Ireland clergyman spoke the following words during a time of intercession in Belfast. In view of their origin, they are as surprising as they are encouraging. They seem to suggest that the second rain will fall in a particularly heavy way in the Catholic Church. Part of the prophetic message reads:

> "The Lord has been shaking the Roman Catholic Church. He holds the church in the palm of His hand and he has been shaking it for 20 to 25 years. The church has been rattling around like a nut in a nutshell. All the time the Lord has been shaking it from the outside. Now He is going to work on the inside. He throws the church down and cracks it open. A holy and pure church is exposed, what was hidden before can now be seen. As the church, broken, flows out, the Glory of God flows in, like a river of liquid gold... This will spread through the Catholic Church infrastructure worldwide, producing great love and devotion for the Lord. For the Glory of God to come

it will be enough to be associated with the Catholic Church, to go to a Catholic Church or to be called a Catholic, even to have contact with the Catholic Church through occasional ceremonies such as baptism, confirmation, first communion, marriage, funerals. By identifying with the church you will be giving the Lord permission to manifest His glory."

Motives for desiring the later rain

Why should we pray for the second rain? I think that our motive is very similar to the one mentioned in Acts 4:23-31, namely, the many external and internal problems the contemporary Church is having to overcome. In an address given at a General Audience as early as Nov. 15th 1972, Pope Paul VI suggested that these ecclesial difficulties have a demonic dimension: "What are the Church's greatest needs at the present time? Don't be surprised at Our answer and don't write it off as simplistic or even superstitious: one of the Church's greatest needs is to be defended against the evil we call the Devil." In that same year the Pope said the diabolic threat was internal as well as external. "The smoke of Satan," he warned, "has entered the temple of God." Apparently he was alluding to the sins of Christians, to the devaluation of the moral law, and the growth of moral decadence. One has only to recall the clerical abuse scandals in different countries, to see how right he was. Years later John Paul II referred to a significant external challenge in par. 9 of his apostolic exhortation *The Church in Europe*. He wrote:"European culture gives the impression of 'silent apostasy' on the part of people who have all that they need and who live as if God did not exist."

Intercede for the later rains

As I said in Chapter 1, there is no blessing or growth in the Christian life without preceding desire. The deeper and stronger the desire the greater is the openness to blessing. That principle is echoed in scripture. For instance in Deuteronomy 4:29-30 we read: "But from there you will seek the Lord your God, and you will find him, if you search after him with all your heart and with all your soul." In a more specific way, Jesus said: "If any one thirst, let him come to me and drink. He who believes in me, as the scripture has said, 'Out of his heart shall flow rivers of living water.' Now this he said about the Spirit", Jn 7:37-39.

We need to gather like the first disciples to fervently intercede to God for boldness in preaching the Good News, with associated signs and wonders. In effect we need to pray for a great revival. Pope John Paul II spoke in a poignant way about the faith conviction that needs to inform our intercession: "When every human means seems to fail, believers turn to God... Even when the Christian feels humanly impotent before the tide of evil, he knows that through prayer he can count on the omnipotence of God who does not abandon those who trust in him. Even if human means fail, hope in God never fails." In par. 15 of his letter on *The Divine Mercy* he echoed what he had already written: "Like the prophets, let us appeal to that love which has maternal characteristics and which, like a mother, follows each of her children, each lost sheep, even if they should number millions, even if in the world evil should prevail over goodness…Let us implore God's mercy for the present generation."

I got an insight into what this might involve, in the mid 1970's, when I attended an Ecumenical conference hosted by Cardinal Suenens in Malines, in Belgium. Towards the end of the proceedings he referred to the fact that in some respects the Church resembled Jerusalem at the time of Nehemiah; the walls of its spirituality have been breached, so that the enemy, in the form of the Trojan Horse of worldliness, can be insinuated into its midst by the Devil, in order to secretly disgorge its malevolent and disruptive influences. Then he opened Isaiah 62:6-7 and said it was about the need for persistent intercessory prayer on behalf of the Church. "I have posted watchmen on your walls, O Jerusalem; they will never be silent day or night. You who call on the Lord, give yourselves no rest, and give him no rest till he establishes Jerusalem and makes her the praise of the earth." Our intercession needs to be frequent, intense, associated with fasting, and within a context of worship.

Like Nehemiah of old, we need to call believing Christians to rebuild the breached walls of Christ's Church. We will do this not only by growing in holiness ourselves, but also by means of a New Evangelisation which is anointed by the power of the Holy Spirit and demonstrated through charismatic deeds of power. As Pope Paul VI said in

Evangelisation in the Modern World: "I earnestly exhort you to generously open your minds and hearts to receive a large outpouring of divine gift, the Holy Spirit. May a new Pentecost descend on you so you will be spiritually renewed and continue on a new road to evangelical witness" As this occurs, we will be enabled to experience the new springtime that was often referred to by John Paul II. For instance, in par. 86 of *Mission of the Redeemer* he wrote: "God is preparing a great springtime for Christianity, and we can already see its first signs. In fact, both in the non-Christian world and in the traditionally Christian world, people are gradually drawing closer to gospel ideals and values, a development which the Church seeks to encourage."

Expanding on this notion, Ralph Martin wrote perceptively in the May/June 1999 edition of *Goodnews*:

> "I believe that we are now in a time of visitation. God is visiting us in the ministry of the Pope, in the ministry of Mary (in different apparitions where she warns people) and in many other ways as well. The time of preparation is well advanced. According to the message of John Paul and Mary we are on the verge of a significant action of God, an action that will function as a two edged sword, depending on our preparation and willingness to respond to the prophetic message we are being given. And is it not possible that the fullness of the 'new springtime' will not come until we are first purified through judgment or chastisement, and awakened to the holiness of God."

Conclusion

I believe that for many years now the Lord has allowed the Church to experience a very difficult time of testing, in order to humble and purify it. During that period he has raised up a large number of people who know the Lord, who are deeply committed to him, and who desire to carry out the great command in the demonstration and power of the Holy Spirit. I believe that a time is coming when there will be great disruption and even breakdown in the secular world. It could be the result of such things as economic hardship, war, natural disasters, or a pandemic. However it occurs, it will cause some people to become bitter and disillusioned, and it will cause others to come to their senses like the prodigal son. Like him, they will seek the Lord while he may still be found, Is 55:6. Then those who have been purified and blessed with the anointing of the second rain of the Spirit, will be ready to engage in the New Evangelisation in the demonstration and power of the Spirit in such a way that will not only fulfill the prophecies already mentioned, it will lead to a great harvest of souls for God.

Chapter Four

Fasting from Criticism

Not only have we to overcome the problem of division between the Christian Churches, we have also to tackle the problem of divisions within the Catholic Church. Over the years, Parish Renewal programmes have been used in many Dioceses in America, Britain and Ireland. Writing about their efficacy, Fr.Vince Dwyer once observed that research in Catholic contexts had indicated that mutual distrust between bishops, priests, and lay people was the main impediment to progress. Typically, it was evoked by things such as criticism, broken promises, individualism, and resentments. I'm quite convinced that mistrust is also one of the most corrosive problems afflicting the renewal movements. In this chapter I want to share a way in which it can be overcome.

A number of years ago, I belonged to a large prayer group. At one point, sixteen of the more experienced members decided to form an auxiliary community group which met on a different night. At the inaugural gathering I gave a keynote address which suggested that we should aim to live like the early Christians as depicted in Acts 4:32-36. Through the power of the Holy Spirit they had realised the ancient Greek ideal of friendship by being conformed to the mind and heart of Christ while having all things in common. When I asked for reactions, I was disappointed to find that many of those present thought that this ideal was far too demanding. Happily, however, one of the chief objectors got a word of knowledge. He said, that if we read Sirach 6:14-18, we would get God's perspective on the issue. I quickly found the passage. It was about friendship!

Commitment to stop criticising others

Some time later, during a memorable meeting, one member of the community group read Luke 6:36-39 and shared how this passage, about unconditional mercy, had inspired her. Then she spontaneously knelt on the floor and said: "I promise to refrain from criticising, judging or condemning anyone in this group, either in thought or word. If I break this promise, I will publicly confess my fault and seek forgiveness." There was a stunned silence. Then, one by one, everyone present, freely knelt down and made the same promise.

That Spirit prompted agreement had remarkable effects. Firstly, Jesus assured us that, "whatever measure you use in giving - large or small - it will be used to measure what is given back to you", Lk 6:38. Justifying grace, as we well know, is not the fruit of good works. Although this unmerited gift of God is always freely available to us, we only experience its liberating power in so far as we put aside the scales of justice by refraining from, judging, condemning, or resenting other people while offering them the undeserved gift of our merciful love. Like a sanctuary lamp within, members of the community group continued to be consciously aware of God's saving grace as long as we maintained a merciful attitude.

Trust and praise levels grew

Secondly, our trust levels grew greatly. As a result, we felt more closely united than ever before. We were no longer afraid that anyone would talk or think in a critical way about us, behind our backs. Our community group became a place of psychological safety where each person could blossom, by being his or her own true self.

Thirdly, while we had always been committed to praising the Lord, when we became more united, there was more joy. A new gift of enthusiastic praise was released, one which was both loud and long. Some of our favourite scriptural verses were from Sirach 43:31-34 which encourage people to redouble their praises, because God is more than worthy of all the appreciation we can express.

Growth in spiritual gifts and evangelisation

Fourthly, although we had often desired the gifts of the Spirit, only a few of them had been granted to us. But when we made love our aim by agreeing to fast from criticism and to praise God with conviction, all the gifts described in 1 Corinthians 12:8-10 were poured out on different members of the group, including the gifts of prophecy and healing.

Fifthly, we also found that, as our unity of mind and heart increased, we not only got more opportunities to evangelise as individuals and as a group, but our attempts to spread the good news were more effective. I can remember one parish mission we conducted in the mountains of Tyrone which was anointed from beginning to end, even to the point of miracles. As Acts 4:33 attests, fruitful evangelisation is not only energised by loving communities, they bear experiential witness to the truth of the message that is preached by the way they live in peaceful unity.

Difference between judging and criticising

Over the years I have discovered a number of implications that follow from these points. As soon as I stopped criticising members of my group, in either thought or word, I also found that I began to stop criticising people outside the group such as relatives, workmates, and people in the media. While I may have to judge what they do, I try to refrain from judging them. I have also found that, to stop criticising others, I have had to stop mentally criticising myself. Nowadays, if I make a mistake, I try not to mutter such things as, "you stupid idiot!" Members of any group will inevitably let one another down, either as a result of weakness or malice. In cases like these, it is important to devise ways of resolving conflicts in a constructive manner. For example, every now and then, a trained facilitator could be invited to help the members of the group to talk about their grievances in an open rather than an accusatory way. Ideally, whenever conflicts arise, the members of the group should be willing go to one another to explain how they feel and why. Then, when necessary, forgiveness can be either asked for, or offered.

Be of one mind

St. Paul once wrote, "Dear brothers and sisters in Christ, I appeal to you by the authority of the Lord Jesus Christ to stop arguing among yourselves. Let there be real harmony so that there won't be divisions in the community. I plead with you to be of one mind, united in thought and purpose", 1 Cor 1:10. I know from experience that when the members of Charismatic groups, of whatever kind, have made an agreement like the one mentioned above, it has not only been in accord with the will of God, it has also borne abundant fruit, especially the fruit of effective evangelisation.

Chapter Five

Two Disasters: One Call to Repentance

In recent times, two disasters have made a big impact on the American public, the collapse of the twin towers in New York (2001) and the devastation caused by hurricane Katrina, which wreaked such havoc in New Orleans (2005). When I heard about them I asked, like so many others, why did the God who cares for the birds of the air and the lilies of the field, allow these deadly events to happen? I'm familiar with different attempts that have been made over the centuries, to understand the phenomenon of evil. From a personal point of view I'm attracted to St Irenaeus' theory that we live in the valley of soul making where psycho-spiritual growth would not be possible without the experience of good and evil. While I find his point of view helpful, it still leaves a lot of problems unresolved. For instance, even if one accepts that our characters are forged on the anvil of adversity, do we really need the sheer amount of mind numbing suffering and loss of life that some people have to endure?

The perspective of Jesus

One can seek to understand the twin towers and the hurricane either from the perspective of firm or weak faith in God. This reflection is written with the former in mind. Instead of examining the two disasters from the standpoint of the philosophy of religion, it will try to understand them in the light of a relevant incident in the public ministry of Jesus.

The passage in question records Jesus' reaction to two tragedies, one man made, the other natural, which were analogous in some ways to the twin towers disaster which was the outcome of human malice, and hurricane Katrina which was the outcome of the confluence of a number of natural phenomena. One was an evil that was inflicted, the other, an evil that was endured. "Now there were some present at that time who told Jesus about the Galileans whose blood Pilate had mixed with their sacrifices. Jesus answered, "Do you think that these Galileans were worse sinners than all the other Galileans because they suffered this way? I tell you, no! But unless you repent, you too will all perish. Or those eighteen who died when the tower in Siloam fell on them - do you think they were more guilty than all the others living in Jerusalem? I tell you, no! But unless you repent, you too will all perish." Lk 13:1-5.

TWO DISASTERS: ONE CALL TO REPENTANCE

Scripture scholars say that neither of the incidents mentioned in this passage was referred to in any other part of the bible or the secular histories of the time. Evidently, both of them took place during Jesus' lifetime within a stone's throw of one another in Jerusalem. We know very little about the Galileans who were murdered within the temple precincts. At Passover time, large crowds used to come to Jerusalem to offer sacrifice in the temple. Evidently, during one of the disturbances that often occurred there, Pilate's troops quelled the unrest in a violent way that led to loss of life. Nor do we know much about the tower that collapsed on eighteen unfortunate people. Archaeologists, however, are fairly sure that they have discovered its ruins near the spring of Siloam, cf. Jn 9:7, several metres south of Herod's fortress. We know that Pilate had been trying to improve the water supply to the city and was using some of the temple revenues to finance the project. The Pharisees argued that the men who worked on it were taking money that properly belonged to God. The collapse of the tower of Siloam may have been connected to the construction work nearby. Furthermore, many people would have interpreted the accident as God's punishment for serious wrongdoing.

This harsh interpretation would have been typical of contemporary Jewish thinking, which believed that all suffering was the consequence of personal sin. As Eliphaz said to Job: "Consider now: Who, being innocent, has ever perished? Where were the upright ever destroyed?" Job 4:7. The same belief was evident in the story of Jesus' cure of the blind man, "His disciples asked him, 'Rabbi, who sinned, this man or his parents, that he was born blind?'" Jn 9:2. Jesus surprised the enquirers when he said that the man's blindness had nothing to do with his own sins or those of his parents.

In the Old Testament Job asked, on behalf of countless men and women down the ages, why bad things happened to good people. However, he didn't really come up with a convincing answer. Suffering remained a mystery. There is little or no evidence that Jesus engaged in speculative thinking about the whys and wherefores of suffering, whether inflicted by people or nature. While he was vividly aware of the afflictions of his fellow human beings, especially the poor, he had an unshakable trust, as Matthew 6:26-34 attests, in the goodness and the providential care of God the Father.

As far as the two incidents mentioned in Luke 13:1-5 were concerned, Jesus accepted that although the people who died were sinners, they were no more so than anyone else. In spite of this acknowledgement, it is clear that he rejected the Jewish notion that their suffering was God's punishment for personal wrongdoing. As Joachim Jeremias pointed out in his *New Testament Theology*, "In Luke 13:1-5, Jesus expressly attacks the dogma that misfortune is a punishment for the definite sins of particular people. Rather, suffering is a call to repentance, a call which goes out to all. Whereas his contemporaries ask, "*Why* does God send suffering?," the disciples of Jesus are to ask, "*For what* does God send suffering?" Jeremias goes on to say, "One answer would be, "God allows suffering, in order to summon people to repentance lest they suffer a greater catastrophe." British scripture scholar George Caird concurs. In his commentary on Luke's gospel he says: "To reject the way of Jesus was to choose the path leading directly to conflict with Rome and subsequent catastrophe."

What catastrophe was being referred to? It would seem that Jesus had a strong premonition that if the people didn't change, a terrible time would ensue when mass murder and destruction would come together on a grand scale (see Luke 19:43-44). While this catastrophe was probable, it wasn't inevitable. If the people, like those of Nineveh in Jonah's time, accepted the Good News message about the in-breaking of God's unconditional mercy and love, and turned back to the Lord, disaster could be averted. However, if the people failed to respond, the forces of evil would inevitably take their destructive and inevitable course. No wonder there was such a sense of urgency in the preaching of Jesus. Is it any surprise that he wept over Jerusalem, Lk 19:41, when he could see that the chosen people were not responding to him and his gospel message. As we know, the Lord's prophecy was fulfilled a few years after his death and resurrection. In 70 AD the Romans destroyed Jerusalem, demolished the Temple and murdered between 600,000 and 1,300,000 people. For instance, Titus condemned many Jews to fight wild beasts in the amphitheatre of Caesarea. It could be argued that Jesus was not only in anguish as he anticipated this disaster, he saw it as a symbol of a greater catastrophe, namely that many people would be found wanting in the general judgment.

Disasters as intimations of the end times

Scripture scholars have suggested that the early Christian community, possibly like Jesus before them, saw the destruction of Jerusalem as a metaphor for greater tribulations that would precede the end times, see 2 Thessalonians 2:1-12. As a result, there has been an eschatological dimension to Christian theology ever since. All disasters, great and small, are symbolic intimations of the convulsive end of history which will be followed by the final judgment. The only real catastrophe to worry about, therefore, is to be found wanting on the last day. As Jesus said on one occasion: "What good will it be for a man if he gains the whole world, yet forfeits his soul?", Mt 16:26. On another occasion he remarked in similar vein: "I will show you whom you should fear: Fear him (i.e. God) who, after the killing of the body, has power to throw you into hell. Yes, I tell you, fear him", Luke 12:5.

It seems to me that while Jesus didn't think that the two catastrophes were God's punishment for personal sin, he did see them as the outcome of people being out of harmony with their Creator and *ipso facto* with their own deepest vocation and purpose. Just as lung cancer can be the result of smoking, so evil actions can be the outcome of the psycho-spiritual pathologies that have resulted from alienation from God. But if people wholeheartedly turned back to God and accepted the free, unmerited gift of

God's forgiving love, not only would human society be transformed, even the natural world could be effected. Sometime after the death and resurrection of Jesus, St Paul expressed this intuition in Romans 8:20 when he said: "For the creation was subjected to frustration, not by its own choice, but by the will of the one who subjected it in hope."

A new creation

It is clear that Jesus not only believed in divine providence, he also believed that Spirit-filled believers could be instruments of God's providential purposes by means of loving relationships, deeds of mercy, action for justice, and charisms of power such as healing and miracle working. They are made possible by means of the gift of expectant faith, cf. 1 Cor 12:9. We can recall how, full of the Spirit, Jesus was able to effect the natural world when he calmed a storm, Mk 4:39, turned water to wine, Jn 2:1-11, caused a fruitless fig tree to wither, Mk 11:20 etc. He wanted to share this same power with those who believed in him. "I tell you the truth, anyone who has faith in me will do what I have been doing. He will do even greater things than these, because I am going to the Father", Jn 14:12-14. In Mark 11:22-24 he declared: "Have faith in God, I tell you the truth, if anyone says to this mountain, 'Go, throw yourself into the sea,' and does not doubt in his heart but believes that what he says will happen, it will be done for him."

Prescinding from the philosophical, scientific and exegetical problems involved, scripture promises that prayer can effect, not only human events, but natural ones also. As one of the apostles wrote: "Elijah was a man just like us. He prayed earnestly that it would not rain, and it did not rain on the land for three and a half years. Again he prayed, and the heavens gave rain, and the earth produced its crops" Jm 5:17-18. In the context of this reflection on two recent disasters, one the result of an act of war, the other an act of nature, I'm reminded of something that Our Lady is reported to have said to Mirjana, one of the visionaries of Medjugorje, "You have forgotten that through prayer and fasting you can avert war *and suspend the laws of nature* (my italics)."

Some implications

As a result of these brief reflections we can come to some tentative conclusions. Firstly, when we experience disasters whether small or large, man made or natural, they are not sent by an angry God, as punishments for sin. That said, they can be the direct or indirect consequence of a lack of relationship with God and a wilful disregard for the guidance of conscience and the Holy Spirit.

Secondly, the different kinds of disaster we experience on a fairly regular basis are symbols of the great crisis that will occur at the end of history when the general judgement will take place. Then the sheep, i.e., the blessed, will enter into eternal glory, while the goats, i.e., the damned, will be cast out into eternal misery.

Thirdly, people should see worldly disasters as invitations

to a repentance that is much needed. I was interested to see that in par. 90 of *Fides et Ratio* (1999) John Paul II spoke about some of the likely consequences of the theistic amnesia that is so common in contemporary culture: "it makes it possible to erase from the countenance of men and women the marks of their likeness to God and thus leads them little by little either to a destructive will to power or to a solitude without hope." In other words, forgetfulness of God leaves people vulnerable to the dark and destructive aspects of their psyches. In Jungian terms, the Evil One exploits irrational human complexes and the destructive aspects of the personal and collective shadow to wreak havoc on the world. In this context we need a change of mind, a turning back to God.

Fourthly, when we are the victims either of different kinds of disaster, or disturbed by the suffering of those that are afflicted by them, we can remember that Jesus himself succumbed to the disaster of passion week. But because he trusted in his loving Father he was vindicated and raised to glory. So when we experience catastrophes, either directly or indirectly, we can be consoled by the thought that Christ enables us to endure in him all that he himself endured and he endures it in us, cf. Col 1:24. But just as his suffering was the prelude to glorious new life, so it will be in our lives. God will use what we endure as a kind of purification that will lead to deeper union with God. In other words, evil does not have the last word, it belongs to God, and it is always a word of blessing and hope.

Fifthly, over the years I have come to appreciate that our Lord's, saying that it is in giving that we receive, Lk 6:38, is a veritable law in the spiritual life. I was interested to see that in the oldest surviving non-apostolic homily (around 100 A.D.), the unknown author says: "Fasting is better than prayer, while charitable giving is better than both, and love covers a multitude of sins." The plight of the victims of 9/11 and hurricane Katrina has evoked an extraordinarily compassionate and generous response from people, not only in the U.S. but all over the world. I'm convinced that this phenomenon is of great spiritual significance. Whether believers or unbelievers, the people are giving in a spirit of love with no strings attached, to strangers they have never met. Surely this outpouring of mercy is prompted, albeit in an anonymous way, by the Holy Spirit. Knowingly or unknowingly, people are responding to the needs of the suffering Christ in the person of the victims, Mt 25:40. Their generosity will call down God's blessing upon the donors. This blessing is likely to contribute to a spiritual springtime yet to come.

Chapter Six

Marriage and the Unequal Yoke

Abraham Maslow, a well known psychologist indicated that human beings are motivated by a hierarchy of needs. Once the basic ones have been satisfied, such as safety, a sense of belonging and self-esteem, people become aware of an inner call, a higher need for self-actualisation. It is mainly satisfied by means of peak experiences, especially of the transcendent kind. In our relatively wealthy, Western society where many basic needs have already been satisfied, there seems to be a growing number of people who are trying to satisfy their higher needs. I saw this in All Hallows College, Dublin, where I used to teach spirituality. Many of my students were middle-aged, married people. For instance, there were a number of men who had opted for early retirement and a number of women whose families had left home. They were motivated by a common desire for a deeper experience and understanding of their Christian faith. They said such things as, "Up to now I have been nurturing others, now it's time to be nurtured myself." I have observed something similar in other Christian groups such as the Charismatic Renewal and twelve step groups. People who attend religious meetings, seminars, conferences and retreats, usually do so in order to mature in their relationship with God, their inner selves and other people.

In this chapter, I want to explore a possible downside of spiritual growth in the lives of married people. I first became aware of this problem many years ago when a male friend of mine talked to me about 'the unequal yoke.' He went on to explain: "If a husband or wife experiences a spiritual awakening and subsequent spiritual growth, it may lead to stress and strain in the relationship with their spouse due to a lack of mutual understanding and communication." I have since come to appreciate what an insightful observation that was. An unequal yoke can take a number of forms. Here are just a few brief examples. Even if they sound a bit artificial they try to get different points across.

Four brief case studies
1. Mary's husband Maurice is a non-church going Protestant with a secular world view. Following her spiritual awakening, many of the experiences Mary shared with Maurice seemed like incomprehensible gobbledygook to him. As St Paul explained: "The man without the Spirit does not accept the things that come from

the Spirit of God, for they are foolishness to him, and he cannot understand them, because they are spiritually discerned", 1 Cor 2:14. When Mary told me about her communication problem, I began to appreciate just how lonely and painful it can be when one's partner cannot empathise with one's cherished spiritual experiences, values and beliefs.

2. When Damien began to develop in a psycho-spiritual way, he was surprised to find that his new found maturity evoked envy in Dorothy, his wife. In the light of her husband's obvious spiritual growth, she suffered from an unacknowledged feeling of inferiority. Instead of applauding Damien's progress, Dorothy resented it. Unconsciously she made invidious comparisons while seeming to say, "I can see that spiritually you are by-passing me and I hate you for making me feel second best. Why can't you revert to your old, less spiritual, ways, when you were mediocre like me?"

3. Sandra and Paul's neurotic relationship was based on a mutual preoccupation with the satisfaction of unmet personal needs. Instead of saying "I need you because I love you," they implicitly said to one another, "I love you because I need you." This co-dependent type of relationship worked well, as long as the couple remained much the same. But when Sandra began to mature spiritually, as a result of attending a Life in the Spirit Seminar, Paul began to become very uneasy and jealous. He often complained: "I don't know why you have to attend all

those meetings. You are becoming a religious fanatic and neglecting me." On an other occasion she was heartbroken and annoyed when he said. "You can't love God unless you love me enough," which meant in effect that he wanted her to stay at home all the time.

4. When David and Irene married they had a lot in common. But from the beginning Irene was more willing to take the road less travelled, from a spiritual point of view. For his part, David, who came from a dysfunctional family was reluctant to leave his familiar comfort zones. Not surprisingly, they grew apart. Deep down David felt intimidated by the fact that Irene had found a new source of interest and energy outside their marriage. He responded in a paranoid way, as if Irene was having an affair. This kind of irrational reaction led to a number of acrimonious rows. Irene told me that, on one occasion, David felt so unsettled by her new found assurance, contentment, and spiritual insight that he went so far as to ask her: "Are you going to leave me?"

Perspectives

How should a spiritual spouse respond to typical problems like these? Firstly, it is not good to capitulate to a partner's unjustifiable insistence that she or he should abandon their spiritual pursuits. That said, husbands and wives have to make sure that they strike a reasonable balance between their right to foster their spiritual lives and their duty to devote sufficient time to their spouse and family. Sadly, we have all known married people who have used a questionable notion of spirituality as an excuse to escape from demanding domestic obligations. I have even talked to wives who went so far as to say, in a Manichean way, that as a result of visiting a Marian shrine like Medjugorje, they felt that our Lady didn't want them to have sexual relations with their husbands!

Secondly, if a rift develops between a 'spiritual' person and his or her spouse, as a result of psycho-spiritual growth, he or she needs to be cautious when forming a heterosexual friendship with a person who may be on the same spiritual wavelength as themselves. What begins in the spirit can easily end in the flesh (See Matthew 26:41). For spiritual relationships like these to succeed, the married person and his or her soul-friend should keep questions like these in mind. Are we whole-heartedly committed to the Person and will of God? Do we focus our energies on mutual self-disclosure rather than on the physical expression of affection? Are we prepared to share honestly about any sexual feelings that may be present, so that we can adjust to one another in a responsible way? While privacy is necessary at times, are we too secretive about our friendship? Knowing it is easy to be self-deceived, are we prepared to listen to our spouse, trusted relatives, colleagues, or friends when they talk to us about their misgivings?

Thirdly, it is important that those whose spiritual growth evokes a sense of insecurity, resentment, or anger in their spouse, should try to patiently empathise with him or her. Not only can this emotional understanding assuage feelings, such as loss, suspicion and alienation, they can lead an antagonistic spouse to accept and even support their partner's spiritual quest, although they don't necessarily share in it themselves.

Fourthly, traditional spirituality has suggested that there are three identifiable stages of the spiritual journey, the purgative, illuminative, and unitive. A spouse who is growing spiritually, may have moved on to either the illuminative or unitive stages of spiritual growth. That said, it is important that he or she appreciate the fact that instead of not being on the journey at all, their spouse is probably at an earlier stage. Developmental psychology has alerted us to the fact that we are all at different stages where moral, psycho-social and faith development are concerned. Inevitably, the man or woman who is fortunate to have had a graced opportunity of maturing spiritually more than his or her spouse, should accept him or her, rather than criticising them, either for not being on the journey at all, or for not being at the same stage of development as oneself.

It is also important to acknowledge that because of differences in temperament and personality, people have different ways of being spiritual. For instance, some men and women espouse an affective approach to God, where images and symbols play an important role. They often experience consolation of spirit e.g. feelings of joy, peace and hope. Others focus on the will. They are content to lovingly adhere to God in the cloud of unknowing. They often have to endure desolation of spirit, e.g. feelings of absence and aridity. Though quite different in many ways, these forms of spirituality are equally valid. If a husband or wife espouses an affective approach to spirituality, he or she would be mistaken to think their spouse was un-spiritual simply because their spirituality seemed less emotional than their own. One has only to think of the years of inner desolation of spirit endured by Blessed Teresa of Calcutta, to see the truth of this. Spiritual directors are aware of the ironic fact that, sometimes the spouse who complains of having to endure an unequal yoke, is him or herself, the one who is less mature spiritually. Because the complainant has an inadequate view of spirituality, or is at an earlier stage of growth, he or she can fail to appreciate the fact that their spouse has a deeper, but different way of relating to God.

It could also be said that it is commonly assumed that women are more religious than men. That is certainly true where attendance at Church and religious functions is concerned. However, the late Sir Alister Hardy indicated in his ground breaking book *The Spiritual Nature of Man* (1979), that, the percentage of men who reported having had religious experience was much the same as that for women. That said, men are probably less inclined to articulate such experiences in a verbal way. Wives need to keep this point in mind. Just because their husbands do not talk about their religious experiences does not necessarily mean that they do not have them.

Conclusion

I know that some married people are mainly aware of the negative aspects of the scenarios already described, such as loneliness, frustration, and disappointment. While this is understandable; as a more objective observer, I'm convinced that they often fail to appreciate that if one partner changes as a result of repeated infillings of the Spirit, he or she will inevitably influence the other, albeit in an unconscious way. I believe that the apparently 'less spiritual' partner often experiences his or her spiritual aspirations and growth, in a vicarious way, in and through the more overt spirituality of the spouse. So if you have to bear an unequal yoke, accept it, with God's help, as part of the Lord's providential plan, both for you and the one you promised to always love, for better or for worse.

If a husband or wife is married to a spouse who seems to be either un-spiritual, less spiritual, or spiritual in a different way, surely the most obvious manner in which their own spirituality could be lovingly expressed would be in the form of non judgmental acceptance. Believing husbands and wives should pray for their partner. One woman told me that when she attends Mass she often says "Lord I am not worthy... but only say the word and WE shall be healed," meaning herself and her husband. A wife, in particular, would do well to take to heart the following words which St. Peter spoke specifically to women who were married to a pagan husband. Surely, nowadays his words could also be adapted to apply to husbands. "Wives accept the authority of your husbands, so that, even if some of them do not obey the word, they may be won over without a word by their wives' conduct, when they see the purity and reverence of your lives", 1 Pt 3:1-2.

St. Monica could be the patron and exemplar of that approach. Although Patricius, her pagan husband, was not exactly a wicked man, he had a bad temper and was unfaithful to his wife. However, Augustine tells us in book nine of his *Confessions* that his mother's patience was so great that even his father's infidelity never became a cause of quarrelling between them. Monica never stopped trying to gain him for Christ, through the virtues with which the Lord had adorned her, and for which her husband respected, loved, and admired her. Those virtues were like so many voices constantly speaking to him about Jesus Christ. As a result of St. Monica's good example, Patricius was finally converted, one year before his death.

Chapter Seven

Friendship and Ecumenism

A few years ago I attended an ecumenical leaders' meeting in Dublin. At one point we broke into groups and were encouraged to tell our companions how and why we got involved in ecumenical work. It turned out to be a deeply moving time of sharing. It became obvious that each one of us had felt called by God to get involved in the work of reconciliation. I regard that calling to be one of the great graces of my adult life. In this chapter I will focus on one important aspect of my experience of ecumenism.

In the late 70s and early 80s Cardinal Suenens wrote a number of helpful reflections on the charismatic renewal. The second of them, entitled *Ecumenism and Charismatic Renewal: Theological and Pastoral Orientations* was published 1978. It is still relevant. I was particularly impressed by a short section entitled, "The Ecumenism of Friendship." In it, the Cardinal stated that, while ecumenism needs to be tackled in many ways, ecumenical friendships could achieve a great deal. With the help of God's grace, they could bring people together, create a climate of trust, and overcome prejudices. Ecumenical friendships which are humble and practical could hasten the day of final reconciliation.

Then he went on to cite the example of the friendship that united Viscount Charles Halifax (1839-1934), an Anglican, and Fernand Portal (1855-1926) a Catholic and a member of my own Vincentian order. They met on the island of Madeira where Halifax had gone in December 1889, with his son Charles who had TB. At the time Portal was acting as a replacement chaplain. The two men went on many walks together, during which they discussed religious issues. A deep friendship began to form between them. Over a period of time they experienced a growing desire to work together in order to foster union between their respective Churches.

The power of love

In spite of their best efforts there were many frustrations. Halifax was deeply disappointed when the Bull *Apostolicae Curae* declared in 1896 that Anglican orders were null and void. Fr Portal wrote a letter of encouragement to his friend: "In nature nothing gets lost; this is even more true in the realm of the supernatural. A single act of love is more effective in producing infinite reverberations than the displacement of an atom. How many acts of love towards

Our Lord and the Holy Church have not you and your friends made. Sooner or later the entire Church will be shaken. Let us not get discouraged, my dear friend." Some time later Portal founded a journal called *La Revue Catholique des Eglises*. Among other things it explored ecumenical issues. In the Spring of 1908, Cardinal Merry del Val, who had become Pius X's Secretary of State, contacted the Superior General of the Vincentians. He said that Fr. Portal was to be removed from his post and forbidden to publish anything or to speak in public. Clearly, the ecumenist had been suspected of 'modernism.' In a spirit of obedience and love for the Church he abandoned his seminary job and stopped publishing the review.

Friendship remained strong

In spite of many difficulties and the Roman condemnations, the friendship between Fr. Portal and Lord Halifax remained strong. They were ready to grasp any opportunity to continue the official dialogue, which had been suspended. Both of them became friendly with Cardinal Mercier, Archbishop of Malines. Having sought the approval of Rome; Mercier, Halifax, and Portal began organising meetings between Anglican and Catholic theologians in Malines. Progress was slow. However, in a prophetic way, Cardinal Mercier advocated the summoning of a great ecumenical council. Portal wrote in January 1925: "There will be then, I hope, an opportunity to work for the union of the Churches."

Sadly, both Mercier and Portal died the following year. As a result the ecumenical flame began to flicker. It burst into new life, as the Cardinal had hoped, nearly forty years later, at the Second Vatican Council. Shortly before his death, Portal spoke these eloquent words: "Then let me tell the people of my time, as well as those of tomorrow, that there is a way to increase their strength a hundredfold... I am speaking of friendship. A friend, a true friend, is the gift of God, even if what we experience together is simply the sweetness of being united in joy and suffering. But if we encounter a soul who harmonises with our highest aspirations, who considers that the ideal of his whole life is to work for the church, that is, for Jesus Christ, our Master, we become united in our inmost depths. And if it so happens that these two Christians are separated, that they belong to different churches, two different backgrounds, but desire with all their strength and might to knock down the barriers and actively work together to this end, will there be any limits to their power?"

Make friends with members of other denominations

I know from personal experience that those two pioneers provided a reliable template for ecumenical endeavour. Make friends with members of other denominations, do what you think is right, be prepared for opposition, even from the churches, but never lose heart. Fr Portal wrote: "The union of the Churches cannot, in fact, be achieved except by real apostles, in other words people of faith using spiritual means first of all: prayer which is the source of grace; charity which gives understanding of persons, even those from whom we are separated; humility which leads us to accept our defects and our faults. We are all guilty with respect to the Church. That is a certain fact which we must recognise. There, it seems to me, we have the essential elements of all action in favour of union."

Section Two:

Empowered

Chapter Eight

Baptism in the Spirit

As was noted in the first chapter, the Second Vatican Council stated that there were two universal calls, the call to holiness and the call to evangelisation, which are shared by all baptised Christians. In par. 90 of his encyclical letter, *Mission of the Redeemer* Pope John Paul II indicated how holiness and evangelisation are interrelated. "A missionary," he wrote, "is really such only if he commits himself to the way of holiness... every member of the faithful is called to holiness and to mission... It is not possible to bear witness to Christ without reflecting his image, which is made alive in us by grace and the power of the Spirit." The Holy Father returned to this theme in pars. 30-31 of *At The Beginning of the New Millennium*. This chapter will suggest that neither real holiness or effective evangelisation is possible without what Pentecostals and Charismatics refer to as 'baptism in the Spirit.' Due to the constraints of space I will not examine the scriptural understanding of this phenomenon. It has been ably dealt with in many books and articles.

An historically significant event

On February 17th 1967, a few years after the conclusion of the Second Vatican Council, twenty five students from Duquesne University attended a momentous retreat in The Ark and the Dove Retreat House on the outskirts of the city. Kevin and Dorothy Ranaghan have described their state of mind in this way, "There was something lacking in their individual Christian lives. They couldn't quite put their finger on it, but somehow there was an emptiness, a lack of dynamism, a sapping of strength in their lives of prayer and action. It was as if their lives as Christians were too much their own creation, as if they were moving forward under their own power and of their own will. It seemed to them that the Christian life wasn't meant to be a purely human achievement." Each of the people who attended the retreat read David Wilkerson's *The Cross and the Switchblade*, the first four chapters of the Acts of the Apostles, and asked for a new outpouring of the Holy Spirit. Afterwards they claimed to have experienced a powerful release of the Spirit and his charismatic gifts.

Patti Mansfield has described her experience in these moving words. "I wandered into the upstairs chapel... not to pray but to tell any students there to come down to the (birthday) party. Yet, when I entered and knelt in the presence of Jesus in the Blessed Sacrament, I literally trembled with a sense of awe before His majesty. I knew in an overwhelming way that He is the King of Kings, the Lord of Lords. I thought, "You had better get out of here quick before something happens to you." But overriding my fear was a much greater desire to surrender myself unconditionally to God.

I prayed, "Father, I give my life to you. Whatever you ask of me, I accept. And if it means suffering, I accept that too. Just teach me to follow Jesus and to love as He loves." In the next moment, I found myself prostrate, flat on my face, and flooded with an experience of the merciful love of God... a love that is totally undeserved, yet lavishly given. Yes, it's true what St. Paul writes, 'The love of God has been poured into our hearts by the Holy Spirit.' My shoes came off in the process. I was indeed on holy ground. I felt as if I wanted to die and be with God. The prayer of St. Augustine captured my experience: 'O Lord, you have made us for yourself and our hearts are restless until they rest in You.' As much as I wanted to bask in His presence, I knew that if I, who am no one special, could experience the love of God in this way, anyone across the face of the earth could do so."

This Pentecostal event fulfilled the prophetic promise implicit in the description of the nature and role of the charisms mentioned in 1 Corinthians 12:8-10, in par. 12 of the *Dogmatic Constitution on the Church*, and par. 3 of the *Decree on the Apostolate of the Laity*. Since then, I myself, like over 100 million Catholics all over the world, have been blessed to share the same experience.

A personal testimony

I was ordained in 1971. In the years immediately after that I had an inchoate longing for something. St. Thomas Aquinas says in his *Summa Theologica*: "The object of faith is not the statement, but the reality." Twentieth century poet T.S. Eliot echoed that sentiment when he wrote in *Choruses from 'The Rock,'* "the endless cycle of idea and action brings... knowledge of words, and ignorance of the Word." My head was stuffed with theology, statements about God, but I was out of touch with the Reality that those statements signified. I suspected that I was suffering from a famine of the experience of the Lord.

In February 1974, I was invited to attend a retreat in the North of Ireland. One of the talks was given by a Church of Ireland clergyman. He spoke about Jesus as the source of our peace. Quite frankly, his inspired words moved me to tears. I wanted to know the Lord the way this man did. Afterwards a nun introduced me to him. We had a brief chat and arranged to meet privately. When we did, I told the clergyman that I was looking for a new awareness of God in my life. He read a memorable passage from Ephesians 3:16-20. It asks that the seeker, "may have power, together with all the saints, to grasp how wide and long and high and deep is the love of Christ, and to know this love that surpasses knowledge - that you may be filled to the measure of all the fullness of God." Then the clergyman prayed for me, firstly in English, then in tongues. Suddenly, and effortlessly I too began to pray fluently in tongues. I knew with great conviction that Jesus loved me and accepted me as I was. I knew what St. Peter meant when he wrote: "Though you have not seen him, you love him and even though you do not see him now, you believe in him and are filled with an inexpressible and glorious joy", 1 Pt 1:8. May I say in passing, that ever since that mystical event I have had a conviction that Baptism in the Spirit is, above all else, a movement from statements *about* God's unconditional love for each one of us, to a personal experience of the reality *of* that incomprehensible love. As William Barry, S.J. has observed, in *Paying Attention to God*, "If I do not know in my bones that God loves me with an everlasting love, I will not dare to open myself to his gaze and to seek to see myself as he sees me."

During the following months and years the inner effects were obvious. It was as if the risen Jesus had walked through the walls of my body to live within me, cf. Gal 2:20. Prayer was easy, scriptures a revelation, my fears were lessened, I had greater ability to love, and exercise the spiritual gifts. Baptism in the Spirit, I discovered, is not so much a one off blessing, as the beginning of a process, one that has been deepened and strengthened by subsequent in-fillings of the Holy Spirit over the years. As a result, it has strengthened my desire to be holy and to evangelise in the name of the Lord.

Is Baptism in the Spirit truly Catholic?

I suspect that many Catholics are wary of the notion of Baptism in the Spirit. Some admit, "I do not even know what the phrase means," others ask, "if it is all that important, how come we never heard about it when we were growing up?" Still others wonder whether baptism in the Spirit is a Protestant notion, or a purely Pentecostal or Charismatic one. Here is a brief response to each objection.

The word baptism in English comes from Greek and means 'to immerse,' i.e., to soak, inundate, or saturate. In other words, to be baptised in the Spirit, means to be filled with the Spirit, cf. Eph 5:18. As John 1:33 shows, there is nothing new about the phrase 'baptised in the Spirit.' It is significant that Jesus used a similar phrase before his ascension into heaven when he said to the apostles, "John baptised with water, but in a few days you will be baptised with the Holy Spirit", Acts 1:5. While it is true that in modern times, Charismatics have drawn attention to the importance of this blessing, it is necessary for every Catholic who wants to fulfill the Church's universal call to holiness and evangelisation.

The Irish bishops referred to its ability to foster holiness when they said in par. 7 of a pastoral letter entitled *Life in the Spirit* that baptism in the Spirit is: "The outpouring of the Holy Spirit is a conversion gift through which one receives a new and significant commitment to the Lordship of Jesus and openness to the power and gifts of the Holy Spirit." Speaking about the infilling of the Spirit the American Bishops said a few years ago in a document entitled, *Grace for a new Springtime*: "The grace of Baptism in the Holy Spirit is two-fold. It is first and foremost a coming to a living awareness of the true reality of Jesus Christ, as the Son of God." Unfortunately, although many Catholics believe that Jesus is the Son of God, and that he died for the forgiveness of sins, they do not have a deep personal relationship with Him as the One who has dethroned their egos so as to reign at the very centre of their lives. When people are baptised in the Spirit, it is as if the risen Jesus walks through the flesh of their bodies to live within them. As a result of knowing in an experiential way that "God has poured out his love into our hearts by the Holy Spirit, whom he has given us" (Rom 5:5), they have a new found desire to treat others the way they would like to be treated themselves, an increased ability to pray, a deeper insight into the spiritual meaning of the scriptures, a desire to be holy, and a growing urge to evangelise.

Secondly, the American bishops say that baptism in the Spirit results in "an increased docility to the Holy Spirit and his power and gifts." The word docility in English comes from a Latin one which refers to a willingness to be taught inwardly by the Spirit. When people are filled by the Spirit, they move from being merely motivated by such things as laws, customs, duties, obligations, and selfish impulses, to being inspired by the promptings of the Holy Spirit. When people are aware of being led in this way, cf. Gal 5:18, they may feel that what they are being asked to do is beyond their natural power and ability. But as a result of baptism in the Spirit, they come to realise that God's power is made perfect in their weakness, and that they can do all things with the help of the One who strengthens them, Phil 4:13.

As Paul observed, "it is God who works in you (by his Spirit) to will and to act according to his good purpose", Phil 2:13. Not only does the Spirit strengthen them in this way, when necessary, he may give them supernatural gifts such as healing, miracle working, and an ability to prophecy , cf. 1 Cor 12:8-10.

Baptism in the Spirit in the lives of the saints

When one reads the lives of the saints it becomes pretty obvious that many of them described religious awakenings that seemed to be similar to present day descriptions of baptism in the Spirit. I will briefly mention three out of many possible examples.

St. Patrick (390-460), the apostle of Ireland, tells us that he was not gospel greedy as a teenager in Roman Britain. He wrote: "I did not believe in the living God from my childhood." However, when he was brought to Ireland as a captive he experienced a crisis. In the midst of his afflictions he began to have a heartfelt desire for a revelation of God. Speaking about his subsequent religious awakening he said: "I cannot hide the gift of God which he gave me in the land of my captivity. There I sought him and there I found him. The Lord made me aware of my unbelief that I might at last advert to my sins and turn wholeheartedly to the Lord my God." As a result of his conversion and religious awakening, Patrick says: "More and more my faith grew stronger and my zeal so intense that in the course of a single day I would say as many as a hundred prayers, and almost as many at night." Time and time again in his *Confessions*, he mentions how the Spirit guided and empowered him in ordinary and extraordinary ways. Not only did he grow to be exceptionally holy, he evangelised a nation. His description of his conversion and its lifelong effects seems to be a description of baptism in the Spirit and its effects.

St. Louise de Marriliac (1591-1660), who founded the Daughters of Charity with St Vincent de Paul, described a life changing spiritual awakening she experienced during the celebration of the Eucharist, on Pentecost Sunday, June 4th 1623. It is a striking fact that ever afterwards, she had an unusually strong devotion to the Holy Spirit. It would be no exaggeration to say that it lay at the heart of her spirituality. Over the years she often came back to the subject of the Spirit and the part it played in her life. For instance, she stated her intention of reflecting each morning on the role of the Holy Spirit in her own life. She wrote: "Reflecting on my lowliness and powerlessness, I shall invoke the grace of the Holy Spirit in which I shall have great confidence for the accomplishment of his will in me, which shall be the sole desire of my heart." On another occasion she said: "Let us pray that Our Lord Jesus Christ may bestow his Spirit upon us, so that we may be so filled with his Spirit that we may do nothing or say nothing except for his glory and his holy love ... O Eternal Light, lift my blindness! O Perfect Unity, create in me simplicity of being! Humble my heart to receive your graces. May the power of love which you have placed in my soul no longer stop at the disorder of my self-sufficiency which, in reality, is but powerlessness and an obstacle to the pure love which

I must have as a result of the indwelling of the Holy Spirit." Not only did Louise grow in holiness, together with St. Vincent de Paul she engaged in the evangelisation of the poor of her day.

St. Therese of Lisieux (1873-1897) said in her autobiography that from the age of four to fifteen she was moody, oversensitive, immature, and inclined to cry a lot. Then at midnight mass, on Christmas Eve 1886, she had a life changing religious experience. She called it her night of conversion and illumination. "Charity had found its way into my heart," she declared, "calling on me to forget myself and simply do what God wanted of me." I feel confident in saying that Therese had experienced what Pentecostals and Charismatics refer to as baptism in the Spirit. Afterwards, she said that as a result of this spiritual awakening: "I felt a great desire to work for the conversion of sinners." It is significant that besides being canonised because of her holiness she was designated a patroness of the missions because of her zeal for souls.

Differing interpretations

Although there are similarities in the way people recount their experiences of baptism in the Spirit there are many individual differences e.g. for some it is sudden and dramatic, for others it is more gradual and gentle. Furthermore, when theologians reflect on such experiences they adopt different approaches e.g. baptism in the Spirit is the release of a grace already given in baptism and confirmation, or a new outpouring or effusion of the Spirit. They can also emphasise different scriptural and historical points. As a result, there are different ways of understanding baptism in the Spirit and how it fits into the more general context of the sacramental and missionary life of the Church.

As Frank D. Macchia indicates in his excellent *Baptised in the Spirit: A Global Pentecostal Theology*, the Pentecostals were the first Christians in the modern era to talk about baptism in the Spirit. They described two blessings, firstly, salvation and sanctification as a result of water baptism, and secondly, power to witness to one's faith, together with charismatic signs, especially tongues, as a result of baptism in the Spirit. James Dunn pointed out in his book *Baptism in the Holy Spirit,* that while Catholic and Protestant scholars would not doubt the genuineness of Pentecostal's experience of the Spirit, they would question the way they interpret it from a scriptural and theological point of view.

The writings of eminent Catholic scholars such as Frs. Frank Sullivan, Raniero Cantalamessa, Killian Mc Donnell, and George Montague indicate that there are two main ways of understanding baptism in the Spirit. Firstly, many of these scholars maintain that baptism in the Spirit is the conscious release, manifestation, and appropriation of dormant graces already received in the sacraments of baptism and confirmation. This thesis was first proposed in Cardinal Suenens's *Theological and Pastoral Orientations of the Catholic Charismatic Renewal.* It has been adopted and developed by many theologians since then. McDonnell and Montague indicated in their book *Christian Initiation and Baptism in the Holy Spirit: Evidence from the First Eight Centuries,* that when adults were being baptised in the early Church they expected to be baptised in the Spirit and to receive one or more of the charisms. They concluded that this special grace is *integral* to the sacraments of initiation and *normative* for all Christians. They write: "Because it belongs to the church as an integral element of Christian initiation, it must be taken with utter seriousness. Indeed the baptism in the Spirit is normative." If their interpretation of the scriptural and patristic data is correct, their conclusion has vital implications for the renewal of the contemporary Church. For example, many Catholics believe that as adults we need to appropriate in a conscious way, the graces we first received in a sacramental manner in baptism and confirmation. This happens as a result of claiming those sacramental graces by means of personal faith. Otherwise they tend to remain inactive rather than active in our lives. As I already mentioned, in par. 51 of his letter, *Lord and Giver of Life* (1986), Pope John Paul II explained, "faith, in its deepest essence, is the openness of the human heart to the gift of God's self-communication in the Holy Spirit.

Frank Sullivan, S.J. published an influential article in *Gregorianum*, entitled, 'Baptism in the Holy Spirit.' Speaking of this grace he said that it was "a religious experience which initiates a decisively new sense of the powerful presence and working of God in one's life, which working usually involves one or more charismatic gifts." While not denying that, ultimately, all Christian grace has its origin in the sacraments of initiation, he said that St. Thomas taught in the *Summa Theologica*, that when people experience an infilling or effusion of the Spirit, such as baptism in the Spirit, God lives in them in a new way, in order that they might do a new thing, such as working miracles, prophesying, or offering their lives as martyrs. In this understanding, baptism in the Spirit is not so much a one-off event, but rather the initiation of an on-going process that allows for new in-fillings of the Spirit which deepen and strengthen the life of grace and witness.

There is reason to believe that the two views of baptism in the Spirit are complementary rather than contradictory. This religious experience is rooted in the graces received in the sacraments of initiation, but besides releasing their potential, there is reason to think that something new, such as the charisms listed in 1 Corinthians 12:8-10 is added. It has often struck me that when Jesus was baptised in the Spirit in the Jordan, and the apostles and the disciples were inundated by the Holy Spirit in the upper room, not only did they experience the love of God being poured into their hearts, cf. Rm 5:5, they were also empowered and gifted to witness to that love. Whereas, Jesus did not seem to have preached or performed any deeds of power before his baptism, he did so continuously afterwards. It was the same with the first Christians. Following Pentecost they began to proclaim the reign of God's liberating mercy and to demonstrate its presence by means of the more remarkable charisms, such as healing and miracle working.

Fr. Peter Hocken has made it clear in a number of his writings, most recently in two *Goodnews* articles entitled 'Baptism in the Spirit: A Biblical Understanding' (Sept/Oct 2007) and 'Baptism in the Spirit: A Catholic Approach' (Nov/Dec 2007), that he is not impressed by either of the approaches outlined above. He feels that they are not sufficiently rooted in scripture. He maintains that the coming of the Spirit at Pentecost and, as a result, all subsequent sendings, have an eschatological dimension in so far as they are an anticipation of the second coming of Jesus at the end of time. He has written: "The implication of the biblical data is that Jesus has come to baptise in the Holy Spirit. This He begins to do after His resurrection and ascension. This immersion in the Holy Spirit is to prepare the way for the coming King and His rule in righteousness. In this light, we should understand the outpouring of the 20th century as a sign of the Lord's coming in glory. That does not mean we have any idea of God's precise timetable."

It could be added by way of addendum that baptism in the Spirit could be considered as a sacramental, like exorcism, cf. *Catechism of the Catholic Church* par. 1673. In par. 1677 of the Catechism we read: "Sacramentals are sacred signs instituted by the Church. They prepare men to receive the fruit of the sacraments and sanctify different circumstances of life." Par. 1670 explains: "Sacramentals do not confer the grace of the Holy Spirit in the way that the sacraments do… For well-disposed members of the faithful, the liturgy of the sacraments and sacramentals sanctifies almost every event of their lives with the divine grace which flows from the Paschal mystery of the passion, death, and resurrection of Christ. From this source all sacraments and sacramentals draw their power." Arguably, when believers lay hands on people, or anoint them with blessed oil, while praying that they be filled with the Spirit, it is a sacramental, and is thus related to sacramental grace.

How to receive the baptism in the Holy Spirit

How does a person become baptised in the Holy Spirit? In my experience, three things are necessary. Firstly, he or she needs a wholehearted desire for this grace. Sometimes it takes months and even years for the desire to deepen and strengthen to such a point that the personality is sufficiently open to receive the un-merited gift of the outpouring of the Spirit. Jesus stressed the importance of desire when he said, "If anyone is thirsty, let him come to me and drink. Whoever believes in me, as the Scripture has said, streams of living water will flow from within him." By this he meant the Spirit, whom those who believed in him were later to receive. Up to that time the Spirit had not been given, since Jesus had not yet been glorified", John 7:37-39.

Secondly, it is important to rely on the infallible promises of God to send the Spirit to those whose desire prompts them to ask for it. Here is just one of many possible New Testament examples. In Luke 11:13, Jesus said to parents, "If you then, though you are evil, know how to give good gifts to your children, how much more will your Father in heaven give the Holy Spirit to those who ask him!" As Catholics, we pray to Mary, the mother of Jesus, to be worthy of this mighty promise of Christ.

Thirdly, it is important to be willing to remove obstacles to the Spirit's coming. Needless to say, all un-repented sin is a barrier, but I have found that the greatest single block is unforgiveness and resentment. So it is important to ask for God's help to remember who it is, living or dead, who still needs your forgiveness. As Colossians 3:13 says, "Therefore, as God's chosen people, holy and dearly loved, clothe yourselves with compassion, kindness, humility, gentleness, and patience. Bear with each other and forgive whatever grievances you may have against one another. Forgive as the Lord forgave you."

Fourthly, people should ask to be baptised in the Spirit with real expectancy. There are many gifts we could ask of God, without being certain that they were in accord with the divine will. But to ask to be filled with the Holy Spirit is always in accord with the centrality of God's will. As scripture assures us: "This is the confidence we have in approaching God: that if we ask anything according to his will, he hears us. And if we know that he hears us - whatever we ask - we know that we have what we asked of him",1 Jn 5:14-15. As soon as people begin to ask for the sending of the Spirit, they receive a first installment of that grace. At the outset they may not be consciously aware of any inner change. But then, either suddenly or gradually, their relationship with Christ will deepen as a result of a religious awakening and thus become more intimate at a conscious level of awareness.

If you wish to ask to pray for an in-filling of the Holy Spirit, begin by answering these questions, "Do you believe that Jesus is the Son of God, that he died to free us from our sins and was raised from the dead to bring us new life? Will you follow Jesus as your Lord?" When you make your profession of faith, say the following prayer with sincerity of heart and expectant trust: "Lord Jesus Christ, I want to belong more fully to you from this time forward. I want to be freed from the power of sin and the evil one. I want to enter more completely into your kingdom to be part of your people. I will turn away from all wrongdoing, and I will avoid everything that leads me to wrongdoing. I ask you to forgive all the sins that I have committed. I offer my life to you, and I promise to put you first in my life and to seek to do your will. I ask you now to drench, soak, and inundate me with your Holy Spirit. I believe that your spiritual hands are upon me and that the red light of your mercy and the white light of your love are flooding my body, mind and soul. I thank you Lord that even as I pray you are responding to my request because it is so in accord with your loving desire for me. Amen."

Baptism in the Spirit and the Eucharist

Some time ago, on the feast of Christ's baptism, I had an unusual awareness as I celebrated Mass. During the Eucharistic prayer, I was thinking of how the Spirit would come down during the words of consecration to transform the bread and wine into the body, blood, soul and divinity of Jesus Christ. Then, I prayed inwardly, "Lord, as you send the Spirit upon the gifts, send it also upon me and the congregation." As I said this, I had a conviction that God was responding. By the time I got to the words of consecration I was so moved with emotion that I could hardly speak. I had a profound sense of the link between the baptism of Jesus in the Jordan and his saving death on the cross. On the day he was revealed to the world as God's anointed Messiah, there was an intimation of the agonies to come for God's suffering servant cf. Is 42:1. Jesus fulfilled that vocation when he willingly laid down his life for all mankind cf. Rm 5:6-8. When he could breathe no longer, he gave a loud cry and said, "Father into your hands I *commit my spirit* (my italics)", Lk 23:46. So at the very moment of his death, Jesus yielded up the breath of the Holy Spirit so that it could be given to all of us. As I blessed the bread and wine I had a heartfelt sense that the same Spirit was coming, simultaneously, upon the gifts, the congregation, and myself in a transforming way. So whenever we celebrate the Eucharist, all of us can earnestly ask, in the words of the third Eucharistic Prayer, "Grant that we who are nourished by his body and blood, may be filled with his Holy Spirit."

Conclusion

This long chapter began by suggesting that holiness and evangelisation are intimately interlinked. While it is true that baptism in the Spirit has been rediscovered by the

Pentecostal and Charismatic movements, it has always been a gift for all the Church. As the booklet *Fanning the Flame*, observes: "accepting the baptism in the Spirit is not joining a movement, any movement." In another publication McDonnell and Montague add: "It is not – as viewed by many today – an optional spirituality in the Church such as... the devotion to the Sacred Heart or the stations of the cross. The baptism in the Holy Spirit does not belong to private piety... *it is the spirituality of the church* (my italics)." Because it is so clearly associated with the sacraments of initiation, a concerted effort is needed, when preparing candidates for baptism and confirmation, e.g. during RCIA courses, to encourage them to expect the Holy Spirit to come upon them with such power that they will receive, not only the gifts mentioned in Isaiah 11:2, but also those mentioned in 1 Corinthians 12:8-10. Empowered by the Spirit and his gifts, Catholics will be enabled by means of the new evangelisation to bring about the new springtime, spoken about by Pope John Paul II, in par. 86 of *Mission of the Redeemer*. "God is preparing a great springtime, for Christianity," he observed, "and we can already see its first signs."

Chapter Nine

Mary and Pentecost

It is a pity that when many of us joined the Charismatic Renewal our devotion to Our Lady was often weakened by a new found devotion to Jesus and the Holy Spirit. Over the years however, equally many of us have found that our love of Mary has re-asserted itself and matured. Now it expresses itself in new ways as we have come to better understand her role in our lives. This has helped to counter balance some of the exaggerated devotions and teaching about her that have been an obstacle to Christian unity. As Paul VI said in par. 32 of *Marian Devotion*, "every care should be taken to avoid any exaggeration which could mislead other Christian brethren about the true doctrine of the Catholic Church." Catholic Charismatics have helped to highlight Mary's role as the archetypal disciple and model for the Church because she was so docile to the power and guidance of the Holy Spirit. In this short chapter I will focus on how she demonstrated that docility and openness throughout her life but particularly at the time of Pentecost.

St. Luke, the author of a Gospel and the Acts of the Apostles, emphasised the role of the Spirit both in the birth of Jesus and the Church. Catholics believe that, not only was Mary conceived without original sin, she remained sinless throughout her life. When the angel Gabriel announced that she was to be the mother of Jesus he said: "The Holy Spirit will come upon you, and the power of the Most High will overshadow you", Lk 1:34-35. There was a clear intimation of Pentecost in that incident and the visitation. When Mary went to help her pregnant cousin, we are told that as soon as Elizabeth heard her greeting she "was filled with the Holy Spirit", Lk 1:41, and spoke in an anointed way about the Mother of God. Then Mary, the spouse of the Spirit, responded in a prophetic manner when she proclaimed her Magnificat.

What was Mary doing in the upper room?

Once the infancy narrative was complete, Luke did not mention Mary again in his gospel. The next time he referred to her was in chapter one of Acts. We are told that, before his ascension, Jesus urged the apostles to go back to Jerusalem to await their baptism in the Holy Spirit. Luke informs us that the apostles together with Mary, and the disciples, "all joined together constantly in prayer", Acts 1:14. This raises the question, what was Mary's role during those days of waiting? We know that the Apostles had a profound sense of failure as a result of deserting Jesus during his passion.

He had predicted that this would happen. On one occasion he had said: "Simon, Simon, Satan has asked to sift you as wheat. But I have prayed for you, Simon, that your faith may not fail", Lk 22:14. In the upper room the disciples were still filled with the same fear that had led to their unfaithfulness. No doubt, Mary moved among them encouraging each one not to loose heart. She would have reminded them of her Son's promise, "blessed are those who mourn (on account of their failures) for they will be comforted", Mt 5:4. She would have assured them that the promised Holy Spirit, the comforter, would be God's answer to the cry of their broken, grieving, longing hearts.

Besides encouraging the apostles and doing thoughtful acts of service such as helping to prepare meals, Mary united herself to her Son's prayer by interceding for the disciples. As the *Constitution on the Church* says in par. 59, "we also see Mary by her prayers imploring the gift of the Spirit, who had already overshadowed her in the Annunciation." Understood in this sense, Mary was the midwife of the Spirit. She, who had given birth to Jesus, prayed constantly for the outpouring of the One who would give birth to the Church whose image, model and mother she was destined to be.

If Mary was full of grace, why did she need to be filled with the Holy Spirit?

Those prayers were answered in a dramatic way on

Pentecost Sunday. Like the many disciples, Mary was inundated with the power and gifts of the Spirit. Just as the believers praised God and spoke in tongues, so did she. In view of the fact that she was full of grace, why did Mary need to be filled with the Spirit? The same question could be asked about her divine Son's baptism. What new grace could He have received on that occasion? Pope Paul VI said that when Jesus was baptised, God's love, which was present from the first moment of His Incarnation, "was manifested in a new way." It is not entirely clear whether it was manifested to Jesus as a human being, to the onlookers, or to both.

Something similar probably happened to Mary. Not only was the length and breadth, the height and depth of God's incomprehensible love manifested to her in a more profound manner than ever before, the Spirit also led her into a deeper understanding of her Son's words, deeds and mission. Although the scriptures do not tell us what she did after Pentecost, surely, Pope John Paul II was correct when he said in one of his Wednesday teachings: "In the nascent Church she passed on to the disciples her memories of the Incarnation, the infancy, the hidden life and the mission of her divine Son as a priceless treasure, thus helping to make him known and to strengthen the faith of believers." In other words, like the apostles, she evangelised in the power of the Spirit.

In Mary the Church sees its own potential for holiness

What the Church says about the action of the Holy Spirit in the Church is what it has already said about Mary. In her, the Church sees its own potential for holiness. However, that has not yet been fully realised. Speaking about the Church's greatest requirement, Pope Paul VI said on Nov 29th 1972: "The Church needs her perennial Pentecost, she needs fire in her heart, words on her lips, prophecy in her outlook. She needs to be the temple of the Holy Spirit… she needs to feel rising from the depths of her inmost personality, almost a weeping, a poem, a prayer, a hymn – the praying voice of the Spirit." Be assured that, as Mother of the Church, Mary is vividly aware of this urgent need. When we say the third glorious mystery of the Rosary we can remember that. From her place in heaven, our Lady continues to pray that the wounded Body of her Son might be renewed by a fresh outpouring of "the Lord and giver of life," and thereby empowered to engage, ever more effectively, in the New Evangelisation.

Chapter Ten

Guided by the Spirit

I must admit that, like many men, I am fascinated by mechanical gadgets such as radio controlled watches, hand held computers, MP3 players and the like. My current favourite is a satellite navigation system, known as a GPS (i.e. a global positioning system). This computerised gadget is used by people who travel by road. They enter their departure point and destination into the GPS. It works out the best way of getting there with the aid of satellites orbiting above the earth. It has a twofold ability to offer guidance. Firstly, an arrow offers precise visual directions on a coloured map which is displayed on a screen. Secondly, a woman's voice gives specific instructions. If perchance the driver makes a mistake, the mellifluous voice graciously suggests an alternative way of getting to the destination, without a hint of criticism. Since purchasing a GPS, I have rarely consulted a map for directions or got lost.

It has struck me on a number of occasions that the Holy Spirit is a bit like a spiritual GPS. It can give those who are tuned into its inspirations the guidance needed for the journey to God. If perchance we make a mistake or ignore its promptings, the Spirit doesn't condemn us. Rather it suggests an alternative way of reaching our destination. No wonder St Vincent de Paul said: "Think of God's guidance more than your own weakness... remain always dependent upon his guidance. Have recourse to him everywhere and in every encounter. Throw yourselves into his arms, recognising him as your loving father, completely confident that he will help you and bless your work." In my youth I was very much attracted by the following prayer for divine guidance, which was written by Cardinal Mercier.

> "O Holy Spirit,
> Beloved of my soul, I adore You.
> Enlighten, strengthen, guide, comfort and console me.
> Tell me what I ought to do and command me to do it.
> I promise to be submissive in everything that you permit
>   to happen to me,
> only show me what is Your will, and give me the grace
>   to do it."

I had no peace

A few years ago, I was sitting at my desk thinking of nothing in particular. Suddenly the thought came spontaneously into my mind, why not write a new prayer, which would be a modern alternative for Mercier's prayer for guidance. My immediate reaction was to say yes. I felt it would be a relatively easy thing to do and wouldn't take long. So I set to work, thinking I'd complete the task in a day or two. In the event it proved much more difficult than I had ever anticipated. I wrote one draft after another. But none of them satisfied me. Pages were repeatedly scrunched into a ball and thrown into the wastepaper basket. Many was the time I thought to myself, "why am I putting myself through all this hassle. After all no one asked me to do this!!" Then I'd abandon the project for a while. But I would have no peace. So I'd have to go back to it again. This went on for months. I lost count of all the versions of the prayer I wrote. None of them really satisfied me. At one point I published a provisional version, in the now defunct *New Creation* magazine, and asked the readers for their feedback. Having taken their replies into consideration I wrote yet another version. I still was not entirely satisfied with it.

Stepping out in faith

But believing that if a thing is worth doing, it is worth doing badly, I brought it to a local printer intending to get 500 copies. I was shocked when he told me how much each one would cost. But he added. "if you got 5,000, the price for each one would be proportionately cheaper." Although I thought it would take years to sell them, I decided to think big, and ordered the larger number.

A few days later I collected the box of new prayer cards and returned to All Hallows College where I was living at the time. As soon as I came through the front door I was greeted by a priest and a lay woman, who were standing in the foyer. They asked, "Are you Fr. Collins?" I said that I was. "We heard you were writing a daily prayer to the Holy Spirit," they explained, "and we have come to see if we could buy some." I said that, by a remarkable coincidence, I was returning from the printers and that the box in my arms was full of the prayer cards. "How many copies would you like?" I asked. "Well, to start with we would like 1,000 copies" replied the priest. I nearly dropped the box with surprise. He wanted exactly twice the number of cards I had originally intended getting printed. That was many years ago. Since then I have sold well over a quarter of a million copies. Thank God, they're still in demand. Every now and then I order a reprint.

I have been encouraged to find that many people have told me that saying the daily prayer to the Spirit has helped to kick start their prayer lives which had often withered away. Furthermore, they said that it helped them stop focusing only on their own needs by helping them to focus on God's will which is expressed in the form of divine inspirations.

Signs of the Spirit

I learned a number of important lessons from that experience. Firstly, if one responds to a God given prompting, it will be associated with inner consolation as long as one follows it. Secondly, when an impulse is prompted by God, it will invariably bear fruit. Thirdly, whereas, a GPS offers mechanical guidance, the Holy Spirit gives spiritual guidance in many ordinary ways such as a holy desire, a twinge of conscience, an inner prompting, or a revelatory word of scripture. He can also guide us in charismatic ways such as a religious dream, vision, prophecy, or word of knowledge. One way or the other, we are enabled, like Jesus, to be "led by the Spirit", Lk 4:1, and to "be guided by the Spirit", Gal 5:18.

So why not say the following daily prayer to the Holy Spirit which is said in the morning. There is an evening prayer also which is not included here. For further reflection on guidance and discernment see chapter nineteen.

> *"Father in heaven, your Spirit, is a Spirit of truth and love.*
> *Pour that same Holy Spirit into my body, mind and soul.*
> *Preserve me today from all illusions and false inspirations.*
> *Reveal your presence and your purposes to me,*
> *In a way that I can understand.*
> *And I thank you that you will do this*
> *While giving me that ability to respond*
> *Through Jesus Christ our Lord. Amen."*

Chapter Eleven

Faith and the Word of God

When I was baptised in the Spirit, well over a quarter of a century ago, I received a new love and understanding of Scripture. Two verses have exercised a big influence on me. The first recounts words which were spoken by God the Father to humanity, "this is my Son whom I love, *Listen to Him* (my italics), Mk 9:7. The second was spoken by Mary at the marriage feast at Cana, "His mother said to the servants, *"do whatever he tells you"* (my italics), Jn 2:5. As a result of pondering verses such as these I would try and read the scriptures every day and ponder what they meant.

One passage that always intrigued me was the story in the gospel of Mark when Jesus cursed the fig tree. When the apostles go past it some time later they see that it has withered to its roots and are amazed, to which Jesus responds, "Have faith in God. Amen I say to you, whoever says to this mountain, "Be lifted up and thrown into the sea, and does not doubt in his heart but believes that what he says will happen, it shall be done for him. Therefore I tell you, all that you ask for in prayer, believe that you will receive it and it shall be yours", Mk 11:22-24.

This is an incredible promise. Jesus says it - so it must be true, but did I really believe it? When I reflected on it, although I assented to its truth in theory, part of me doubted because I had never actually seen a miracle myself. In academic circles people tend to cope with this dilemma by spiritualising the interpretation so it no longer means what the text says literally. In fact, whenever I brought this point up I would be accused of being a fundamentalist or having an over-excited imagination. I felt in my heart, however, there was more to it than that and I wrestled in prayer with this passage for six months.

The thing with the Word of God is there are two aspects to it. There is an objective truth about the Word, which is true whether you believe it or not, but for the Word to bear fruit in your life, you have to hear it as a revelatory word, and that is always a gift from God which you have no control over. I seemed to be getting no light on it at all, but I kept knocking and the answer came in a way I least expected.

I spoke with more faith about these things than I actually had

At the time I was teaching A level religion in a boys' school. We had a very good football team and had reached the semi-finals of the cup. Then tragedy struck. Our star player injured his back. He could hardly stand straight and was totally out of action. The whole school was devastated. A deputation of boys came to see me and asked me to pray with him so he would get well, reminding me of how often I had talked about the miraculous working of God's power. I felt cornered. The truth was I spoke with more faith about these things, than I actually had. And the boys themselves would often chant 'Jackanory', at me as they didn't believe it. But in this moment of difficulty they were prepared to try anything.

Found it hard to believe

I didn't feel confident enough to pray, so I avoided the issue, by telling them it was up to the boy himself to come and ask me. I used the same excuse when a short time later the headmaster approached me with the same request. But then Hugh, the boy himself turned up and spoke to me directly. "I can't sleep", he told me. "I am in pain all the time. I can't study. Would you pray for me? You are always talking about the power of prayer!"

There was nothing for it. The two of us went into one of the classrooms on our own and I brought my New Testament with me. I asked him if he had faith that Jesus could heal him. He said, "I believe with my mind, but it is hard to believe it is true for me today." I confessed that I was in the same boat and that I found it hard to believe as well, but that we needed to step out in faith.

Pray with the measure of faith you have

I asked him where the pain was. I knew very little about praying for people at the time, but I knew I should say something to his back. I also knew that you should only pray with the measure of faith you have and be honest. I felt sure that God would shine the light of the Holy Spirit on his back if I asked, so I prayed "May the light of your Holy Spirit shine on the vertebrae, disks and tendons that are injured." So far so good. "And may the light of your Holy Spirit command them to yield to your purposes and your will." All this was still within the measure of my faith.

The word dropped from my head to my heart

Then somewhere in the middle of that prayer, the Word dropped from my head to my heart and suddenly I received the gift of faith and experienced a strong conviction that that he would be healed, and prayed accordingly. "Be healed right now," I said. Then I felt led to thank God in anticipation of what I knew He was going to do. I was convinced that something had happened, but when I asked Hugh how he felt, he told me that as I had begun to pray the pain had got more intense. "Look at Jesus," I told him, "not the pain", reassuring him that healing was often not instantaneous but a process.

When I went back to my room, I went down on my knees in desperate intercession, reminding the Lord that it was his honour at stake, all the boys would be watching, and the sports master who had stopped going to Mass had promised to reconsider his position if Hugh was healed. I had never felt so vulnerable and not in control, and I begged the Lord to act.

By the next morning my faith had faltered a great deal and with a heavy heart I went to class. Hugh always sat in the front of the room and I was afraid to ask him any question the other boys could hear. I could see him sitting there, so there was nothing for it and I went up to him and asked him in a whisper how he was. "I'm perfect today," he said. All the boys in class gasped, and for the first time in my life I had the experience of the Word of God going out and not returning to me empty but achieving what it set out to do.

Distinction between ordinary faith and expectant faith

In fact this was not the only healing to come out of it all. The boy's girlfriend told one of the teachers at her school what happened, and advised her to come and see me. When I reluctantly prayed for her, she was healed too. These incidents massively increased my faith, but it clarified for me the distinction between ordinary faith in God and the expectant faith that is necessary for healing and miracles. When we read God's promises in the Scriptures, the mind can give mental assent to God's promises but faith is in the heart and requires a revelatory word, which needs a lot of prayer, and is ultimately a gift from God.

I'm sure it is something the Lord is calling us to do more

often. We really must be prepared to wrestle in prayer with all the magnificent promises God makes in scripture and ask for faith to believe. If we do believe it will bear fruit even to the point of miracles, which is what the Church needs today.

Chapter Twelve

Did Jesus Exercise Faith?

In this chapter I want to reflect, in an exploratory way, on a question which has intrigued me for a long time. While faith is vital in our Christian life, did Jesus have faith? The answer depends on what we mean by faith. In our culture we say a person has faith if they believe that God exists. Clearly, Jesus didn't need to believe in his own existence. Christian faith can refer to the assent of mind and heart to the truths taught by scripture and the Church. Jesus did not have this kind of faith either. Those truths were about himself and the other persons of the Trinity. Christians also talk about saving faith e.g. in Romans 10:9. Obviously, as one who was utterly sinless and divine, Jesus didn't need or have justifying faith. So it would seem that the Son of God did not have faith. St. Thomas Aquinas confirmed this fact when he said in one of his writings, "Faith is the evidence of things not seen." But there was nothing that was not known to Christ, according to what Peter said to Him "You know all things." Therefore there was no faith in Christ."

The New Testament on the faith of Jesus

There is not one single, unambiguous reference to the faith of Jesus in the New Testament. However, there are a number of ambiguous references which imply that he did have faith. For instance, many translations of Hebrews 12:2 read: "look to Jesus the pioneer and perfecter of OUR faith." In the Greek, the word 'our' is not mentioned. The more accurate translation would be: "look to Jesus the pioneer and perfecter of faith." The phrase "perfecter of faith" could refer either to our faith in Jesus, the faith of Jesus himself, or possibly both together. If you read the story of the cure of the epileptic boy in Mark 9:17-29 you will find that the disciples were unable to cure him because of their lack of faith. When the boy's father said that the demonic spirit: "has often cast him into the fire and into the water, to destroy him; but if you are able to do anything, have pity on us and help us," Jesus replied: "If you are able! – All things can be done for the ONE who believes." To whom does the word 'one' refer? to the father? to the disciples? or to Jesus himself? or to a combination of all three? When Jesus casts out the spirit, it is strongly implied that He is the one who has faith.

Did Jesus have the charism of faith?

If Jesus needed faith to exorcise the epileptic boy it would have been the charism rather than the other forms of faith.

It is mentioned in 1 Corinthians 12:9, "To some is given the charism of faith." It is the firm, expectant trust that is needed to perform miracles. Jesus described it very accurately when he said in Mark 11:23-24, "Have faith in God. I solemnly assure you, if you say to this mountain, 'Be taken up and thrown into the sea,' and if you do not doubt in the heart, but believe that what you say will come to pass, it will be done for you." Did Jesus have this kind of faith?

It may come as a surprise to hear that St. Thomas Aquinas implied that the answer was yes. "Christ," he said, "is the first and chief teacher of spiritual doctrine and faith, according to Hebrews 2:3,4... Hence it is clear that *all the gratuitous graces were most excellently in Christ as in the first and chief teacher of the faith* (my italics)," It is worth noting that in par. 4 of his encyclical *Divinum Illud Munus* (1897), on the Holy Spirit, Pope Leo XIII endorsed Thomas' view when he wrote: "In him (Christ)... were all the treasures of wisdom and knowledge, graces *gratis datae*, (i.e. charisms) virtues, and all other gifts foretold in the prophecies of Isaiah." So if we take Thomas' and Leo's words literally, it would seem that they were implying that Jesus did exercise the charism of faith. This gift would have enabled him, among other things, to perform deeds of power such as healings, exorcisms and miracles.

The raising of Lazarus a possible model of faith

It seems to me that we may have an outstanding example of the exercise of such faith, in the raising of Lazarus from the dead, cf. Jn 11:1-45. To exercise the charism of faith a person firstly needs a revelation of God's will. We know that in all things Jesus was led by the Spirit. There is clear evidence that God the Father had made known to him that Lazarus would die and that he would raise him from the dead. As a result Jesus was able to tell the apostles, in a prophetic manner, what was about to happen. When he got to the tomb of his beloved friend the people were wailing and crying loudly in accordance with the Jewish custom of having intense mourning for four days. He was so moved in an empathic way by the sadness of the mourners that he sighed and wept quietly. Besides saying that he felt compassion the Greek text implies that he was angry, not with the mourners, but with death and its ultimate master, the devil. But he knew that it was God's will to reveal His glory by defeating the devil and raising Lazarus from the dead. What Jesus said to his Father at the tomb is really significant. "I thank you for hearing my prayer. I knew indeed that you always hear me." It does sound like an expression of faith, of unhesitating confidence, that God will act in answer to a prayer which is in accord with his will. As he said to St Peter in Mark 11:24, "I tell you, whatever you ask for in prayer, believe that you will have received it, and it will be yours." There is a similar verse in the writings of St. John: "This is the confidence we have in approaching God: that if we ask anything according to his will, he hears us. And if we know that he hears us - whatever we ask - we know that we have what we asked of him", 1 Jn 5:14-15. If Jesus had this kind of faith, as I suspect he had, it was quite remarkable. By now, Lazarus was dead for four days. Jews believed that after the third day, the soul had definitely left the body. The corpse was already in a state of decay. So there is something utterly awe inspiring and majestic about the words that Jesus spoke. "Lazarus, here, come out!" Isaiah 55:11 says: "my word... shall not return to me empty, but it shall accomplish that which I purpose, and succeed in the thing for which I sent it." The words of Jesus contained the power of their own fulfilment. As soon as they were uttered, the Holy Spirit, the Lord and giver of life, raised Lazarus from the dead. It was a mighty miracle, and as a result many of the people who witnessed it, believed in Jesus. It goes without saying that the raising of Lazarus prefigured Christ's own resurrection from the dead after three days in the tomb.

Conclusion

It seems to me that the raising of Lazarus like other miracles of Jesus, seems to indicate that as the Son of God, he is not only the object of our faith, in a qualified charismatic sense, he may also be the model of that faith. Par. 521 of the *Catechism of the Catholic Church* says that "Christ enables us to live in him, all that he himself lived, and he lives it in us." In other words, because the biography of Jesus is our potential autobiography, he can enable us, when God wills it, to live in him the charism of faith which he exercised, by enabling us to occasionally heal the sick, drive out evil spirits, and perform miracles even to the point of raising the dead.

Chapter Thirteen

Rekindling Your Faith

Following on what was said in previous chapters, I would like to share a few thoughts on the meaning of the all important word 'faith'. In Hebrews 11:1 there is a well known definition: "Faith is being sure of what we hope for and certain of what we do not see." Later we read in Hebrews 11:6 that: "without faith it is impossible to please God." There are three forms of faith in the Bible, believing, trusting, and expectant.

Believing faith

Believing faith is giving the assent of your mind and will to truths taught by scripture and the Catholic Church. It could be described as doctrinal or propositional faith. The First Vatican Council had this kind of faith in mind when it said that it was "a supernatural virtue by which with the inspiration and help of God's grace, we believe that what he has revealed is true - not because its intrinsic truth is seen with the natural light of reason - but because of the authority of the God who reveals it."

My late mother was not only widely read, she had a degree in science and a teaching qualification. When we spoke about controversial Church teachings e.g. about artificial forms of birth control or the ordination of women, she would say. "Pat my intelligence and knowledge are limited. I am content to believe whatever the Pope teaches because he speaks on Christ's behalf." That was believing faith.

Trusting Faith

Trusting faith involves a confident conviction about the loving goodness, providence and provision of God. Pope John Paul II had this kind of faith in mind when he said in par. 51 of his encyclical *Lord and Giver of Life*: "faith, in its deepest essence, is the openness of the human heart to the gift: to God's self-communication in the Holy Spirit." Notice that instead of stressing mental assent to the doctrines taught by the Church, this definition, which is like a description of prayer, emphasises trusting receptiveness to the person, promises and inspirations of God. The fundamental way in which this is done is described in par. 15 of the agreed statement between the Catholic Church, the Lutheran World Federation and the Methodist church: "By grace alone, in faith in Christ's saving work and not because of any merit on our part, we are accepted by God and receive the Holy Spirit who renews our hearts while equipping and calling us to good works."

At a more practical level of trust I can remember a doctor recounting how, when he got seriously ill and was confined to bed, he read Psalm 23. He was really struck by verse 2 which says: "He makes me lie down in green pastures." Suddenly, he was inspired to realise that the Lord had allowed him to get sick for a purpose. He had been working and worrying too much. He felt that he needed to change his priorities and to establish a better balance between work and leisure in his life. In other words, he trusted that the Lord had allowed his sickness for a providential purpose.

Expectant faith

Expectant faith is an intense form of trusting faith. It is utterly convinced that God will act in specific circumstances of need in accordance with the divine promises. Jesus spoke about it when he said, "Have faith in God. I tell you the truth, if anyone says to this mountain, 'Go, throw yourself into the sea,' and does not doubt in his heart but believes that what he says will happen, it will be done for him", Mk 11:22-23. The woman with the chronic bleeding problem exercised this kind of expectant faith when she declared "If I touch his garments I *will* get well", Mk 5:24-34.

Recently, a number of us listened to a talk by Patti Mansfield about Padre Pio. At the end, we all had an opportunity to bless ourselves with a first class relic which contained a drop of the saint's blood. One priest, prayed with expectant faith for the cure of his sister's pancreatic cancer. His sister knew nothing about this. A few days later his sister rang him to say that she had gone for a regular checkup. She said that the medical profession were able to confirm that no trace of the deadly disease could be found in her body. She had been healed, praise God!

Growing in faith

In 2 Timothy 1:6 Paul said, "Fan into flame the gift of God, which is in you." This verse summons up the image of a coal fire which has died down and is covered with ashes. However, beneath the ashes the embers still glow with heat. If the ash is cleared away, a bellows can be used to fan the embers into lively flames once again. It is important to note that when St Paul encouraged Timothy to fan into a flame the gift of faith he had received, he did not tell him to ask God to do the fanning. The Lord had already poured the Holy Spirit into his heart. It was up to him to cooperate with that grace by fanning it into a flame by his own graced efforts. When you desire to re-kindle your faith, you need to have the three forms of faith in mind. Each one of them is vitally important.

1) Many Christians are not well acquainted with the teachings of the scriptures and the Church. Unwittingly they may espouse beliefs that are not compatible with either of them. If you want to grow in doctrinal faith, in a way that exposes and corrects mistaken beliefs like these, it is

important that you prayerfully read the scriptures in the light of Tradition, the Fathers of the Church, and the teaching of the contemporary Popes. All of them come together in the *Catechism of the Catholic Church*. To attend a suitable adult education course can be very helpful in this regard. You cannot believe what you do not know.

2) If you want to grow in trusting faith, the idea of God's love for you has to drop the vital 18 inches from your head to your heart. As St Paul prayed: "may you have power to comprehend with all the saints what is the breadth and length and height and depth, and to know the love of Christ which surpasses knowledge", Eph 3:18-19. While baptism in the Spirit often kick starts this awareness it has to be deepened and strengthened by subsequent in-fillings of the Spirit. As you grow in the conviction of God's personal love for you, you will have an increasing sense that, not only has he a providential plan for your life, you will be confident that he will provide you with whatever you need to fulfill that plan. If you mess up because of weakness or willfulness God's plan B, and if necessary plans C, and D, will kick into place. When they do, you will have a conviction that: "where sin increased, grace increased all the more", Rom 5:20.

3) Expectant faith grows by focusing on the God of the promises and on the promises of God. Because we trust in God, we wholeheartedly rely on his promises. For example, Jesus said these infallible words on one occasion: "Therefore I tell you, whatever you ask for in

prayer, believe that you have received it, and it will be yours", Mk 11:24-25. You need to ponder and pray about words like these because as St. Paul assured us: "faith comes from hearing the message, and the message is heard through the word of Christ", Rom 10:17. As Smith Wigglesworth once said: "There are four principles we need to maintain: First, read the Word of God. Second, consume the Word of God until it consumes you. Third believe the Word of God. Fourth, act on the Word." What Paul and Wigglesworth had in mind here, goes beyond the word as an objective truth upon the page of the Bible to refer to the inspired word that jumps alive off the page into the heart, with subjective meaning. As the Lord assures us, this revelatory word, "shall not return to me void, but shall do my will, achieving the purpose for which I send it", Is 55:11. You can also pray to Mary who herself was blessed because she believed that the promise made to her by the angel Gabriel would be fulfilled, cf. Lk 1:45. You could say the traditional words: "pray for me most holy Mother of God that I may be worthy of the promises of Christ."

Conclusion

If you want to help to rekindle the faith of others, you need to grow in faith yourself. So you can pray with the man in the gospel: "Lord I believe, help my unbelief", Mk 9:24. Then it is a matter of giving the example of a life animated by faith, sharing Christian beliefs with people when it seems appropriate, and praying with expectancy that the grace of God will touch their lives in whatever way is desirable.

Section Three: Gifted

Chapter Fourteen

St Thomas Aquinas on the Charismatic Gifts and the New Evangelisation

It may surprise you to know that St Thomas Aquinas (1225-1274), the greatest theologian the Catholic Church has ever produced, wrote a great deal about the charisms in 1 Corinthians 12:8-10. He did so in three main places, the relevant sections of his verse by verse commentary on first Corinthians; in the *Summa Contra Gentiles*; and in a 32,000 word treatise on the gifts in his *Summa Theologica*. Although Thomas produced a detailed theology of the gifts, it is surprising how seldom Catholic Charismatics refer to it either in word or in print. In this chapter, I want to provide a brief summary of his main points.

Sanctifying grace and charismatic gifts
St. Thomas made a distinction between different kinds of

grace. Firstly, there are sanctifying graces *i.e.* graces which make people pleasing in the sight of God. Then there are charismatic graces. Rather than making a person pleasing in the sight of God, they are graces freely given in order to help others to grow in sanctifying grace. Indeed, St. Thomas went so far as to say that it was conceivable that people in the state of mortal sin could be given gifts, such as healing and miracle working, for the evangelisation of others, cf. Mt 7:21-23.

Thomas's classification of the gifts

Scripture scholars have asked whether St. Paul's list of nine gifts in 1 Corinthians 12:8-10 can be classified in any way. Although the apostle probably hadn't any conscious classification in mind, St. Thomas thought, for theological reasons, that they can be divided into three groups: "some of them pertain to knowledge (revelation), some to speech (proclamation), and some to operation (demonstration)." The nomenclature in brackets is mine.

A) Gifts of Revelation

St. Thomas said that revelation was "an inner light of the mind." All the revelatory gifts are rooted in the charism of prophecy which is "a kind of knowledge impressed under the form of teaching on the prophet's intellect, by Divine revelation." Having stated that this knowledge goes beyond the natural powers of the mind, he went on to describe the various ways in which it can be imparted by God, such as images, dreams, visions, and intellectual illumination.

While these are prompted by the Spirit they are mediated by the angels. He said that, often prophecy has to do with future events. One of the ways in which it is exercised is through, what Charismatics refer to as, the word of knowledge. Thomas says that rather than being an aspect of the "utterance of knowledge" mentioned in 1 Corinthians 12:8, the word of knowledge is a form of the prophetic gift mentioned in 1 Corinthians 12:10.

Rapture is the second revelatory gift, cf. 2 Cor 12:2-4. Strictly, speaking it is not one mentioned by Paul in 1 Corinthians 12:8-10. Nevertheless, Thomas says that rapture is a grace whereby "a person is lifted up by the Spirit of God to supernatural things, and withdraws from his senses, as Ezekiel 8:3 says, "the Spirit lifted me up between the earth and the heaven, and in visions of God he took me to Jerusalem." What Thomas says about rapture is reminiscent of what we know about higher states of contemplation. It raises the question, is the contemporary experience, which is variously referred to as 'slaying in the Spirit,' or 'resting in the Spirit,' sometimes a rapture state during which a revelation is received?

Discernment of spirits is the third revelatory gift. Writing about it Thomas said: "To another is given the ability to distinguish between spirits, namely, in order that a man be able to discern by what spirit someone is moved to speak or work; for example, whether by the spirit of charity or by the spirit of envy." It would seem from this quotation, that St. Thomas did not restrict the charism of distinguishing of spirits to prophecy, but widened it to include the testing of any kind of inspiration or prompting.

B) Gifts of Proclamation

Clearly, Thomas believed that the Lord gives people revealed knowledge not only to enlighten them personally, but in order that they might enlighten others by means of verbal evangelisation. He wrote: "Now because those who receive a revelation from God ought in the order of divine enactment to instruct others, there needed to be further communicated the grace of speech."

Consistent with his didactic understanding of the gifts, Thomas clearly interpreted the charism of tongues as *xenoglossi* i.e. an ability that the Apostles received from God of speaking the foreign languages used by their listeners. Thomas knew that for four days St. Dominic, the founder of his Dominican Order, had been enabled to speak German to people he had met on a pilgrimage. Thomas said very little about tongues as *glossolalia*, which according to Paul in 1 Corinthians 14:14, was a gift of private prayer. He gave a curious explanation of the charism of the interpretation of tongues. He said that it is a Spirit given ability to explain difficult scripture verses. He quoted two texts in Daniel 5:16 and Genesis 40:8 to support his view.

Writing about the gifts of wisdom and knowledge cf. Is 11:2, with which he was richly endowed himself, St. Thomas said succinctly, "Knowledge of divine things is called wisdom, and all knowledge of human beings shares the more general term of knowledge." Then he added: "It is significant that the Apostle places in the charismatic graces not wisdom and knowledge, but the *utterance* of wisdom and knowledge, which are gifts with the ability of persuading others by speech about matters pertaining to wisdom and knowledge." Thomas said that the two gifts of utterance become effective by instructing the intellect, moving the listener emotionally, and swaying him or her to love that which has been spoken about in words. Speaking of women he said, in a way that would be questioned nowadays, that they can exercise the gifts of the utterance of wisdom and knowledge in private, domestic situations, but not in public.

C) Gifts of Demonstration
Through the prophetic gifts of revelation, a person gets to know the truths of faith. Through the gifts of proclamation, such as the ability of speaking foreign languages, and to communicate wisdom and knowledge, revelation is imparted to others. But, St. Thomas, says that the trans-rational truth of what is proclaimed needs to be confirmed by the working of deeds of power. "Any proclamation," he said, "requires confirmation before it can be received…The means, therefore, to show that the proclamation of these preachers comes from God was the evidence of works done by them such as none other than God could do, healing the sick, and other miracles."

Thomas appreciated that the charism of faith was the key, not only to effective proclamation, but to healing and miracle working. Writing about the link between charismatic faith and proclamation he observed: "It is not as a virtue justifying man himself, but it implies a supereminent certitude of faith, whereby a person is fitted for instructing others concerning such things as belong to the faith." Speaking about faith and demonstration by means of deeds of power he added: "The working of miracles is ascribed to faith for two reasons. First, because it is directed to the confirmation of faith; secondly, because it proceeds from God's almighty power on which faith relies. Nevertheless, just as besides the grace of faith, the grace of the word is necessary that people may be instructed in the faith, so too is the grace of miracles necessary that people may be confirmed in their faith."

Conclusion

Given the fact that St. Thomas lived in an age when the charisms were not widely exercised, his description of the gifts of the Spirit is not only surprising in its detail, it is a *tour de force* as far as its theological depth and coherence are concerned. I may say in passing that in the 18th century, Pope Benedict XIV wrote a long, but much neglected, treatise on the charisms which was deeply influenced by St. Thomas's writings. It seems to me that Thomas's evangelistic interpretation of the gifts in 1 Corinthians 12:8-10 is tailor-made for a charismatic understanding of the New Evangelisation called for by the Church. Yes, his views need some modification in the light of contemporary scripture scholarship and charismatic experience, but overall his interpretation provides us with a well thought out theology that shows that the proclamation and demonstration of the Good News needs to be rooted in revelation, especially the gift of prophecy.

Chapter Fifteen

Pope Benedict XIV on the Charisms in 1 Corinthians 12:8-10

Prospero Lambertini was born in Bologna in 1675. By the age of 19 he had received doctorates in theology and in canon and civil law. He was so widely read that he was reputed to be one of the most erudite men of his time. He lived in the Age of Enlightenment when the Church was being attacked by rationalist philosophers and challenged by absolutist rulers. In 1712 he was appointed canon theologian at the Vatican and assessor of the Congregation of Rites. In 1731 he became Archbishop of his native city. Later in 1740 he was elected Pope following a consistory which lasted six months! He took the name of Benedict XIV and is considered by many scholars as the most learned Pope the Church has ever had. He died in 1758 at the age of 83.

While he was at the Congregation of Rites, Lambertini had the responsibility of assessing the causes of people who had been put forward for possible beatification and canonisation. It raised the question in the bishop's mind, what criteria should be used? Eventually, he wrote a massive work entitled *On the Beatification and Canonisation of the Servants of God*. In 1850, English scholars translated part of the Latin version into almost unintelligible English and published three volumes with the collective title *Heroic Virtue*. The last of these, mainly dealt with the charisms in 1 Corinthians 12:8-10. Although he was heavily influenced by St. Thomas, he did not classify the gifts as his theological mentor had done. Whereas St .Thomas looked at the gifts in relationship to the universal call to evangelise, Cardinal Lambertini looked at them in relationship to the universal call to holiness, by examining St Paul's list one by one.

Wisdom and knowledge

Lambertini began by acknowledging that 1 Corinthians 12:8 was not referring to the gifts in Isaiah 11:2. Speaking of the utterance of wisdom and knowledge he wrote: "The word of wisdom, then, is the external word of Divine things; by which a man without human study and labour, so discourses of Divine mysteries as to make it manifest that the Holy Spirit speaks in him, and none may contradict him, by whom unbelievers are converted to, and the faithful confirmed in, the faith. And the word of knowledge is nothing else but discourse or speech on moral matters, relating to everlasting salvation, going forth readily without human study and labour, in writing or by word of mouth, where by those who hear it, understand that it proceeds not from human power, but Divine." Having defined how the gifts involve revealed knowledge, he gave examples of the way gifted men and women brought about remarkable changes in their listeners by the power of their anointed words e.g. St. Louis Bertrand baptised 15,000 Indians who had been converted to the faith as a result of his preaching.

Faith, healing and miracles
A) The charism of faith
Unfortunately, Lambertini did not offer his own definition of this charism. He believed that it was a gratuitous grace in virtue of which miracles and healings were performed by people who had firm confidence in God. He wrote, "the grace of faith is nearly identical with the grace of healing and miracle working." He observed that, though related, the gift of faith was separate from deeds of power because they are performed by God to confirm what the person of faith has proclaimed.

B) The charisms of healings and Miracle working
Lambertini also considered the question, how does the charism of healings differ from that of miracle working? He gave a number of answers. Firstly, he did not think that either the charisms of healings, or miracle working, were a permanent endowment. He felt that they were given afresh, by God, on each occasion they were exercised. Secondly, although he thought that healings and miracles were

abundant in the early Church in order to demonstrate the truth of the apostolic teaching, he did not think that they had completely died out afterwards. Like St. Augustine, he was convinced that healings and miracles continued to be experienced in the Church as a result of such things as trust in the sacraments, the use of holy relics and the prayers and ministry of saintly people.

Prophecy

Lambertini devoted no fewer than seventy six pages of his book to the gift of prophecy. He said that, "A prophet, then, is he who foretells future events, or reveals to others things past, or present things hidden; although generally, and for the most part, prophecy is confined to the foretelling of future events." He said that although prophecies are inspired by God, they are often made possible by the mediation of angels. He added: "it is necessary for prophesying that the mind should be raised to the highest contemplation of spiritual things, this may be prevented through violent passions and inordinate attention to outward things."

Having quoted: "Do not put out the Spirit's fire, do not treat prophecies with contempt. Test everything. Hold on to the good" in 1 Thessalonians 5:19, Lambertini went on to suggest three main criteria that could be used in the assessment of a prophecy. Firstly, was it in accord with the teachings of Jesus, the Apostles, and Church law? Secondly, what was the interior state of the prophet when s/he spoke?

False prophets, he observed, speak when their minds are disturbed, because they cannot endure the assaults of the devil, who influences them. But he added: "they whom God moves, speak with gentleness, humility and modesty." Thirdly, "How can we know when a message has been spoken by the Lord?" asked Lambertini, "If what a prophet proclaims in the name of the Lord does not take place or come true, then a genuine message has not been spoken "

The charism of the discernment of Spirits

Lambertini suggested that there were two ways of understanding discernment of spirits. Firstly there is the art of discernment which can be conducted in accordance with rules set forth by people like Evagrius of Ponticus and St. Ignatius of Loyola. Then there is the gift mentioned in 1 Corinthians 12:10. He defined it as follows: "The gift of discerning spirits is therefore nothing else but an enlightening of the mind, with which man being endowed, easily and without error decides from what source his own thoughts and those of others, which are subjects of choice, proceed, what is suggested by a good, or evil spirit."

Speaking in tongues and interpretation of tongues

Bishop Lambertini saw the gift of speaking in tongues exclusively as *xenoglossi* i.e. the gift of speaking an unknown language/s. For example, when the cause of St. Francis Xavier was being examined by the Rota in Rome, the official report said: "Xavier was illustrious for the gift of tongues, for he spoke with elegance and fluency the languages, which he had never learnt, of different nations, to whom he went for the sake of preaching the Gospel, just as if he had been born and bred among them; and it happened not infrequently, that while he was preaching, men of diverse nations heard him speak each in his own language." Unlike St. Thomas he thought that it was possible that the gift of tongues may have referred to an ability of the hearers to understand the foreign language being spoken by the evangelist. For example, he cited the fact that St. Antoninus recounted how this gift was granted to St Vincent Ferrer: "This was astonishing, and an apostolic grace, that preaching in Catalonia in the common language of the country, he was understood by other nations who knew it not."

Given that Lambertini only interpreted the gift of tongues as *xenoglossi*, his understanding of the gift of the interpretation of tongues was necessarily influenced and even distorted by that fact. He said that the charism could be understood in two ways. Firstly, as an ability to translate the foreign words spoken by an evangelist and secondly, the gift might have referred to a graced ability to "teach the mysteries which lie hid in the words."

Conclusion

Because Lambertini had so little personal experience of the subjects he wrote about, he was more like a man writing an article for an encyclopedia or theological dictionary than a creative theologian. Although his work demonstrates immense learning it is not as innovative as the writing of St. Thomas, his great teacher on the charisms. There is an inherent tension in his approach, as there is in St. Thomas. On the one hand, although he was at pains to point out that the exercise of the gifts was not dependant on personal holiness, on the other, he thought the exercise of the charisms could be seen as an indication of holiness in those who lived lives of heroic virtue. In spite of these caveats, Prospero Lambertini's account of the charisms is not only significant, because he later became the Pope, it would also be true to say that, up to the time of Second Vatican Council, it was the most authoritative summary of Catholic teaching on the gifts of the Spirit. If you want to read what Benedict XIV actually said, you can download his book at http://www.archive.org/details/heroicvirtue03beneuoft

Chapter Sixteen

The Mystical Dimension of the Charisms

Fr. Karl Rahner S.J. was probably the best known Catholic theologian of the late 20th century. In the 1970s he wrote: "The Christian of the future will be a mystic or he or she will not exist at all, if by mysticism we mean…a genuine experience of God emerging from the very heart of our existence." This statement is very true and its truth and importance will become still clearer in the spirituality of the future. The passing years have shown just how prescient he was. Not only has sociological research indicated that, in modern Catholicism, the centre of gravity is shifting from the experience of religious authority to the authority of religious experience, Pope John Paul II acknowledged this trend when he wrote: "People today put more trust in… experience than in dogma."

A mystic is a person who goes beyond mere head

knowledge about God, to have a direct, heartfelt awareness of the length and breadth, the height and depth of the love of Christ, (see Eph 3:18-19). Mystic consciousness, whether mild or intense, is a characteristic of religious experience and lies at the heart of all genuine Christianity. Ever since my dramatic spiritual awakening in my late twenties, I have firmly believed that one of the reasons why the Pentecostal and Charismatic Movements have been so successful, is that they frequently have a mystical dimension to their spiritualities. One has only to read about how charismatics have experienced visions, revelations, the gift of tears, and resting in the Spirit, to appreciate that their spirituality has a lot in common with traditional mysticism. In this chapter, I want to draw attention to some of the mystical characteristics of the charisms mentioned in 1 Corinthians 12:8-10.

Wisdom and knowledge – fruit of contemplation

We begin with the gift of the utterance of wisdom and knowledge in 1 Corinthians 12:8. Needless to say these charisms are rooted in the gifts of wisdom and knowledge mentioned in Isaiah 11:2. Writing about these gifts St. Augustine said: "the knowledge of divine things is properly called wisdom, and that of human things is properly called knowledge." St. Ignatius of Loyola once observed that "it is not much knowledge that fills and satisfies the soul, but the intimate understanding and relish of the truth." In other words, the kind of wisdom and knowledge that leads to anointed preaching and teaching is the fruit of contemplation rather than merely academic effort. I must confess that there have been blessed occasions while preparing or delivering homilies when I have felt that I was being actively inspired by the Spirit. As Jesus promised in John 14:25, "The Counsellor, the Holy Spirit, whom my Father will send in my name, he will teach you all things." That promise finds an echo in 1 John 2:27, "As for you, the anointing you received from him remains in you, and you do not need anyone to teach you. But as his anointing teaches you about all things and as that anointing is real, not counterfeit - just as it has taught you, remain in him."

Charisms of Power – experiential manifestation of the glory of God

Paul goes on in 1 Corinthians 12:9-10 to list the charisms of healings and miracle working which depend upon the charism of faith. I suspect that this latter gift is rooted in the charisms of wisdom and knowledge. It enables a person to go beyond a notional belief that God might perform a healing or miracle, to have a here-and-now conviction that God is already beginning to do so. Those who have been granted this supernatural surge of expectant faith know that it is a mystical type of awareness, one that puts the person in direct union with the mind and will of God. More often than not, it leads either to a confident prayer of intercession or to an expectant prayer of command. Sometimes, such a prayer may be accompanied by a physical feeling of energy trickling down one's arm, accompanied, perhaps, by heat in one's hands. I can remember one such occasion when I was praying for a sick woman. I was overwhelmed by a sense of the awesome presence of God. It evoked mixed feelings in me. I was so palpably aware of the holiness of the Lord that I felt unworthy to be in the divine presence. At the same time, I found the Lord so fascinating, that I desired to draw even closer to him. When people either experience a healing miracle, or witness one, it is an epiphany, an experiential manifestation of the glory of the Lord. Some time ago, I was present when Damian Stayne prayed for a disabled woman. When she got up from her wheelchair and walked, there was an audible gasp of amazement in the hall, and we spontaneously thought to ourselves, "surely, God is among us here!" (1 Cor 14:25).

Prophecy – result of divine revelation

In 1 Corinthians 12:10 St. Paul writes about the gift of prophecy. Arguably, it is the most important charism because of its ability to build up the Christian community. A prophecy is the result of divine revelation rather then the action of the human mind. It can come in at least three different ways. Firstly, there is foreknowledge of future events e.g. Smith Wigglesworth telling David du Plessis in 1937 (see chapter three), that God would use him to spread the doctrine of Baptism in the Spirit in the mainline churches. Secondly, there is the prophetic word of knowledge, a gift whereby a person is granted a supernatural revelation of facts about a person or situation, which could not be learned by the efforts of the natural mind. Kathryn Kuhlman was famous for her ability to know who was being healed, of what ailment during her healing services. Finally, prophecy, can take the form of reading hearts. Both the Cure of Ars and Padre Pio exercised this gift. Among other things, they could tell people about their secret un-confessed sins. Having had occasional experiences of the three forms of prophecy, I know that they are particularly mystical. One has a feeling of being intimately united to God. Through the action of the Spirit, who searches everything, including the depths of God, one has a feeling of sharing in the mind and heart of Christ, (see 1 Corinthians 2:16). I may say in passing that the gift of discernment of spirits, mentioned in 1 Corinthians 12:10, is a practical ability, rooted in the gifts of wisdom and knowledge, which enables a person to ascertain whether a prophecy is truly from God or not. In my experience, it is the least mystical of all the charisms. For more on this see chapter nineteen.

Tongues – pre-rational prayer

Finally, in 1 Corinthians 12:10 Paul mentions the charisms of tongues and the interpretation of tongues. In my book, *He Has Anointed Me*, I pointed out that the charism of praying in tongues, whether in the form of praise, quiet adoration or anguished intercession can have a contemplative, quasi-mystical quality. I say this because it enables the loving will to focus on the mystery of the One who surpasses understanding, without the assistance of thoughts or images. Praying in tongues has a lot in common with the kind of centering prayer, of a contemplative kind, described by the Fathers of the Church e.g. John Cassian. This pre-rational form of prayer prepares the soul to receive revelation from the Lord e.g. in the form of dreams, visions, inner promptings, revelations and the like. Sometimes a prophecy will be uttered in tongues. In such cases it needs to be interpreted, see 1 Corinthians 14:13. Usually, the interpretation comes in the form of an image, scripture text, or prophecy. In so far as such interpretations are inspired by the Spirit they can have a mystical aura.

Mystical dimension needed in the Church

While I'm well aware that a person can exercise the charisms without being in the state of grace, nevertheless, I'm convinced that those who do exercise them, often find that they unite them closely to the Lord. I could honestly say that some of my most mystical moments have occurred while ministering to others by means of the gifts of the Spirit. Nowadays this mystical dimension is much needed in the mainline churches, many of which are losing their members because of arid rationalism. When contemporary Christians are baptised in the Spirit and exercise the gifts of the Spirit, they are enabled to have a mystical sense of God's loving presence. As Karl Rahner wrote: "The spirituality of the future... will have to live much more clearly than hitherto out of a solitary, immediate experience of God and his Spirit in the individual."

Chapter Seventeen

Healing and the Eucharist

In spite of its frequent breakthroughs, modern medicine is unable to cure many ailments of mind or body. As suffering people discover this, it is not surprising that they not only turn to alternative forms of therapy such as acupuncture, homeopathy, and reflexology, they sometimes resort to some of the more esoteric forms of New Age healing in the hope that they will bring them relief. Many of the same people are devout Christians who attend church on a regular basis. While they expect to receive spiritual help from the sacraments, normally they are not encouraged to expect healing of mind or body. For example, during services for the anointing of the sick many homilists rightly stress the comforting power of the sacrament while failing to emphasise its healing potential. Not surprisingly, therefore, many suffering people look for non-sacramental forms of healing. They travel to Marian shrines such as Lourdes or Fatima, seek out relics, go to healers, pray to

Padre Pio, and so on. Although there may be nothing necessarily wrong with these approaches to healing, it is a pity that the official church has sometimes failed to recognise or to promote the healing power of its sacraments. In this chapter I would like to concentrate on the eucharist in particular, in order to highlight its ability to bring healing not only to the human spirit but to mind and body as well.

A memorable experience

A few years ago I conducted a retreat for some lay people in London. On the final day we had a sharing session. Toward the end, Lucy, a middle aged woman told us her remarkable story. Apparently she had entered a convent when she was eighteen. Then the night before her final profession, she upped and left without telling anyone. Although she felt terribly guilty about her impulsive departure, she never returned. Some time later she fell in love and married. Tragically her first child died shortly after birth. Lucy believed - quite mistakenly of course - that God was punishing her for abandoning her religious vocation. She continued to believe this, in spite of the fact that her second child survived and enjoyed good health. As the years passed her unresolved sense of guilt led to different kinds of neurotic problems. She developed severe agoraphobia. Because she was afraid of going outdoors she became a virtual prisoner in her own home, unable to visit friends, attend church, or to do her shopping. This went on for about fifteen years.

Eventually Lucy was so anxious and depressed that she decided to take her own life. She saved up lots of pills with the intention of taking an overdose. Then one day in a state of despair and desperation she left her house and walked down the street in a daze. As she passed her parish church some primordial instinct drew her inside. Mass was in progress. Lucy knelt at the back of the main isle. A silent scream of inner pain welled up inside her. By now the priest had reached the consecration. As he extended his hands over the gifts he called on the Holy Spirit to descend upon them. At that very moment Lucy felt as if a bolt of lightening had hit her. A surge of energy passed through her body. She experienced a physical sense of heat and tingling. This went on for a few minutes. By the time it began to die down Lucy was a changed woman. Instead of feeling a sense of morbid guilt, she felt loved and cherished by an incredibly merciful God. Not only that, her depression had lifted, her agoraphobia had disappeared and she felt an inward sense of peace and joy. It was as if she had been born again. In fact she was so changed by this dramatic experience that, for a time, her husband found her hard to cope with. Instead of being dependant as heretofore, she was now self-possessed and confident.

Jesus brings good news

After hearing Lucy's remarkable testimony, I reflected on its spiritual and pastoral implications, in the belief that it would enable me to deepen my appreciation of the healing power of the Eucharist. The first thing that occurred to me was the fact that the extension of the priest's hands over the gifts was reminiscent of the Old Testament notion of the scapegoat. This curious ritual was associated with the Day of Atonement when one of two goats, that had been chosen by lot, was sent alive into the wilderness. In Leviticus 16:21-23 we are told that a priest would bring "a live goat and laying hands upon its head, confess over it the sins of the people of Israel. He shall lay all their sins upon the head of the goat and send it into the desert....and so the goat shall carry all the sins of the people into a land where no one lives" Meantime the other goat was sacrificed.

Later in the Old Testament the prophet Isaiah pointed, in a prophetic way, to Jesus as the definitive scapegoat. The sins of the people would be laid on him, he would carry them on their behalf so that they might be forgiven. "The Lord has laid on him the iniquity of us all… the righteous one my servant, shall make many righteous", Is 53:5;11. St. Paul echoed this sentiment when he wrote: "For our sake God made him to be sin who knows no sin, so that in him we might become the righteousness of God", 2 Cor 5:21. However, Isaiah went beyond the teaching of the Book of Leviticus which had merely stressed the scapegoat's ability to carry away the sins of the people. The Suffering Servant would also bear the sufferings and diseases of the people that they might experience healing of mind and body. "Surely he has borne our infirmities and carried our diseases, " writes the prophet, "and we have been healed by his bruises", Is 52:25. Later St. Peter echoed these words when he wrote: "Through his bruises you have been healed", 1 Pt 2:25.

When finally he came, Jesus was motivated by compassion to proclaim the good news of God's merciful love. Not only were the ordinary people of his day oppressed from a human point of view, they also felt cut off from God. They were unable to carry the heavy yoke of the law which had been laid upon their shoulders by the religious authorities in Jerusalem. Jesus was anointed by the Spirit to show God's love to the poor who felt that they had fallen hopelessly short of what the Lord expected of them. He said that God's salvation and liberation were at hand. The Lord was breaking into their lives and was pouring out his unconditional and unrestricted love. The debt of sin was being cancelled. All the people had to do was to look trustingly into the eyes of God's mercy, expecting only mercy and they would receive only mercy.

As one who bore witness to the loving mercy of God, Jesus was also motivated by compassion to demonstrate the truth of his proclamation, by performing deeds of power, such as healings, exorcisms and miracles. Perhaps he was aware of a saying of Hanina Ben Dosa, one of his contemporaries, who maintained that: "He whose deeds exceed his wisdom, his wisdom shall endure, he whose wisdom exceeds his deeds, his wisdom shall not endure." Not content with proclaiming the Good News of the Kingdom in his preaching, Jesus witnessed to it by performing healings, exorcisms and miracles. As St. Peter was to say of him: "You know about Jesus of Nazareth and how God poured out on him the Holy Spirit and power. He went everywhere doing good and healing all who were under the power of the devil, for God was with him" (Acts 10:38). In his book *Healing and Christianity* Morton Kelsey has written: "If Jesus had one mission it was to bring the power and healing of God's creative, loving Spirit to bear upon the moral, mental and physical illnesses of the people around him."

Jesus as God's bandage

Jesus' desire to proclaim and demonstrate the good news of God's saving love came to a poignant climax when he was crucified. Some time ago when I was reflecting on this mystery of salvation I recalled an occasion in my childhood when I got a nasty wound in my leg. I had been climbing a tree. A branch broke and a piece of wood stuck into my thigh muscle. As soon as I got home my mother removed it and dressed the wound. Some time later, my father a veterinary surgeon, made a poultice which was designed to draw out the infection while disinfecting the damaged tissues. In the event it was very effective. Then it occurred to me that Christ, our scapegoat, is the poultice of God. He not only enfolded our woundedness on the cross, he continues to do so. It is moving to think that Christ, the innocent One, was in a sense willing to absorb the evil of our sin and suffering into himself. On Calvary this unparalleled act of compassion was symbolised by the darkness that enveloped him as his life blood ebbed away, " It was now about noon, and darkness came over the whole land until three in the afternoon" (Lk 23:44). It was as if Christ absorbed into himself all that alienated us from God and personal wholeness, as he sank firstly into the dark night of the soul and secondly into *sheol*, the shadowy dwelling place of the living dead. As he did so he offered us the wonderful balm of his forgiveness and healing.

The Eucharist and healing

Over the years I have become increasingly convinced that in the Eucharist Jesus wants to bless those who suffer in two interrelated ways. He wants to offer healing to all by either *helping* or *curing* them.

A) Healing as Help

God can offer healing by helping people who suffer to see the true spiritual meaning of the things they endure. Pope John Paul II has described what they might come to understand. "By his suffering and death Jesus took on himself all human suffering, and he gave it new value. As a matter of fact, he calls upon the sick, upon everyone who suffers, to join him in the salvation of the world... This truth is very hard to express accurately, but St. Paul put it this way, 'in my flesh I complete what is lacking in Christ's afflictions for the sake of his body, that is, the Church'", Col 1:24. Once the Lord has revealed truths like these to the heart, he strengthens those who suffer either in mind or body by enabling them to willingly bear their crosses with patience, courage and even cheerfulness. Scripture says that this ability has two beneficial effects. Firstly Romans 5:3-5 tells us that it fosters Christian virtues: "We rejoice in our sufferings, knowing that suffering produces endurance, and endurance produces character, and character produces hope. Secondly, 2 Corinthians 1:3-5 says that suffering can school a person in compassion: "God...comforts us in all our affliction, so that we may be able to comfort those who are in any affliction, with the comfort with which we ourselves are comforted by God."

B) Healing as Cure

In some mysterious instances Jesus in the Eucharist is willing to heal some people by curing their mental or physical afflictions. Why this is so, we can't pretend to understand. Perhaps the cures we experience now are an encouraging sign and foretaste of the total healing that will occur when Christ comes again in glory. What we do know is that God is willing to cure people. This occurs for some of them when they receive the Eucharist with expectant faith. Their need and the Lord's willingness to heal is often expressed in the readings and is especially clear in the prayers of the communion rite. From a subjective point of view there are certain points that are worth focusing on because they can strengthen faith in the healing power of the Eucharistic Jesus.

Holy Communion and healing

It is clear that the healing power of the Eucharist is most evident in the prayers that preceded holy communion. We will look at five instances.

1) The opening words of the Lord's Prayer, "Hallowed be thy name", Mt 6:9 is not primarily about what we do for God, i.e. praising his holy name, but about what God does

for us i.e. by manifesting his majesty, holiness and saving power. In Ezekiel 36:23 we read: "I will hallow my great name which you have profaned among the nations." God does this, pre-eminently, by ushering in his kingdom, hence the next petition, "Thy kingdom come." While these petitions refer primarily to the end times when Christ will come in great glory, they also ask that God would begin to inaugurate the final victory in the here and now, not only by forgiving sins, but also by healing people.

2) Later in the Lord's Prayer we ask the Father to "Deliver us from evil", Mt 6:13 , i.e. to free us from the power of Satan the evil one. In other words we are asking God to free us from any non-human form of evil that would try to separate us from God. It is arguable that some of the destructive tendencies we see at work in people's lives, e.g. a compulsive desire to commit suicide, may be due not just to severe depression but also to the malign promptings of the enemy of our souls. The scriptures remind us: "For our struggle is not against flesh and blood, but against the rulers, against the authorities, against the powers of this dark world and against the spiritual forces of evil in the heavenly realms", Eph 6:12. Pope John Paul II has drawn attention to the fact that the evil one not only tempts individuals but whole nations. He said on one occasion: "Dear sons and daughters...your country seems to be living again the temptations of Christ...Satan, the tempter, the adversary of Christ, will use all his might and all his deceptions to win your people for the way of the world...Pray, pray not to be led into temptation...Pray that

you may not fail in the test. Pray as Jesus taught us to pray: 'Lead us not into temptation but deliver us from evil."

3) Having completed the Lord's Prayer we go on to say: "Protect us from all anxiety." Nowadays many people lead stressful lives as a result of the pace and pressure of modern living. Indeed it has been said, with some justification, that we live in the 'Age of Anxiety'. In his *Introduction to the Devout Life*, St Francis de sales maintains that: "With the single exception of sin, anxiety is the greatest evil that can happen to a soul." Interestingly, the word anxiety comes from the Latin meaning to 'to press tightly, to narrow' and is related to the English words 'anguish' and 'angina'. Psychologists have indicated that many of our anxieties can be traced back to childhood e.g. to a fear that we will lose the love, approval and acceptance of our carers. Because they are inclined to be mistrustful, anxious people are often self-absorbed. To a greater or lesser extent, they tend to be narrow minded and defensive where new ideas and relationships are concerned, including relationship with God. Ronald Rolheiser has suggested that when we pray "protect us from all anxiety" we really mean: "Protect us Lord, from going through life with a chip on our shoulders, angry at the world, full of paranoia, looking for someone to blame for our unhappiness."

4) Just before receiving holy communion we pray the following two prayers. Firstly we say, "Lamb of God you take away the sins of the world: grant us peace." *Shalom* was the Old Testament word for peace. It referred to

anything that enjoyed integrity, completeness and wellbeing. *Erine* was the New Testament term for peace. It referred to the tranquil possession of good things, happiness and above all health. So when we pray for peace, we ask, not only for reconciliation with God and our neighbour, but also for wholeness of mind and body. Secondly, we go on to say in the words of the Roman Centurion: "Only say the word and I shall be healed" (Mt 8:8). Many priests and lay people maintain that this petition refers to spiritual healing only. They are mistaken. The Lord wants to heal us as persons, in spirit, mind and body. The Church indicates that this is, indeed, the case when it directs the celebrant to pray quietly: "Lord Jesus, with faith in your love and mercy I eat your body and drink your blood. Let it not bring me condemnation, but health in *mind* and *body.*"

Experiencing eucharistic healing

If you go to mass with a need for healing, it is necessary that you admit this to yourself while at the same time revealing it to the Lord in prayer. Tell him of your desire for emotional and psychological integration, deliverance from addictive behaviours and attitudes, and also for relief from physical ailments and disabilities. Allow these needs to become an aching, sighing longing within you, one that reaches out to touch the hem of the Lord's presence in the Eucharist. Then when you receive the Eucharist, Jesus can become a mystical bandage wrapping himself around your woundedness. He can soak in your sin and give you his mercy, absorb your weakness and give you his strength, assimilate your brokeness and give you health in mind and body. Finally, you might pray: "If what I ask is not in accord with your will or for your greater glory, I for my part am content to accept whatever is in accordance with both."

Eucharistic cures can occur in a number of ways. Because the mass is pre-eminently a sacrament of love that calls you to live a life of love, the priest may assure those who are present that if they are suffering from any inner hurt or emotional problem that would impede their ability to love, the Lord would want to heal it. Presuming that you are consciously aware of some such problem - after all they are very common - you could bring the painful memory or dysfunctional emotional attitude to the Lord while asking him to touch it with his healing power. Surely, he would want to do this. St. John writes: "Our fearlessness towards him, consists in this, that if we ask anything in accordance with his will he hears us. And if we know that he listens to whatever we ask of him, we know that we already possess whatever we have asked of him", 1 Jn 5:14-15.

The Lord can cure a person as he or she receives holy communion. For example, a few years ago I discovered that a woman who was attending a workshop I was conducting had been suffering from a severe depression for years. Although she had received the best of medical treatment she hadn't recovered. Well, on the Saturday night we celebrated the vigil mass of Sunday. Before distributing holy communion I encouraged those present to believe that the Lord wanted to heal any emotional problems that might inhibit their ability to love. When the depressed woman came forward to receive, a lay minister of the Eucharist handed her the chalice and said to her, "Susan, this is the blood of Christ, may it bring you healing." At that very moment, she became inwardly convinced that her depression was being lifted and that her hurting emotions were being healed. Immediately she began to feel better. Her recovery was rapid, complete and permanent. She hasn't suffered from depression from that day to this.

Sometimes after the distribution of communion, the celebrant will pray for the healing of various ailments. This can be done in three different ways. Firstly, if people have told him about their physical and emotional problems he can pray for them one by one. For example, he might say: "We are praying for the woman who suffers from stress and migraines ...the man with arthritis in his left hip" and so on. Secondly, the priest can pray for the alleviation of different physical conditions in a systematic way, beginning with the head and working down to the feet, or *vice versa* e.g. "We are praying now for those who suffer from bad sight... poor hearing etc. Thirdly, the celebrant can adopt a more spontaneous approach. He could begin by asking the Lord for guidance while going on to pray on the basis of intuitions and hunches which may come to him in the form of images e.g. seeing a swollen elbow. He also might get an intellectual sense about what disease the Lord might want to cure e.g. lupus or cancer of the bowel.

I had the privilege of celebrating the final mass at a

national charismatic conference in Athlone, during which I spoke about the healing power of the Eucharist. When the mass was over and most people had headed off home an English woman approached me. She had travelled to Ireland to attend the conference. She told me that she had suffered from a painful form of arthritis for many years. During the Eucharist, as she trusted in the healing power of Jesus ,she experienced heat going through her body. She said with joy in her face, "Father, I have no pain at the moment, I think that I have been healed."

Conclusion
As the Church rediscovers the healing power of the sacraments, especially the Eucharist and the Anointing of the sick, it will add credibility to its proclamation of the Good News of God's saving Love. As Frank McNutt wrote: "If we preach the power of Jesus to save and redeem the whole person, people want to see that power made real." While it is a good and worthwhile thing for pilgrims to go to such places as Lourdes and San Giovanni Rotondo, I dream of a day when people will not have to travel to far away places in search of a cure. All they will have to do is to attend the Eucharist in their own local church in order to experience the healing power of the Lord. If a prayer like the following, from the mass of healing, is offered, anything could happen. "Lord, through your gift of the Spirit, you bless us, even now, with *comfort* and *healing*, strength and hope, forgiveness and peace... Father accept this offering from your whole family, and especially those who ask for

healing of body, mind and spirit. Grant us peace in this life, save us from final damnation and count us among those you have chosen." As prayers like these are answered, perhaps we will get used to seeing such things as crutches, spectacles and hearing aids hanging on the walls of our churches. They will act as tangible reminders of the great things the Lord has done in accordance with his promises. As one poet wrote: "We are wrapped and swathed round in dreams, dreams that are enigmatical, and the future comes not true save through these."

Chapter Eighteen

Three Types of Discernment of Spirits

Those of us who are members of the Charismatic Movement are familiar with the charism of discernment of spirits in 1 Corinthians 12:10. However, it is not the only form of discernment. This chapter will suggest that in fact there are three interrelated forms of Christian discernment.

The charism of discernment
In 1 Corinthians 12:10 St Paul mentions the charism of discernment of spirits. In his commentary on this text, scripture scholar George Montague maintains that it is a Spirit-given ability to recognise whether a prophecy which is uttered by somebody in the community is truly from the Lord or not. For example, at charismatic prayer meetings people will occasionally claim that God has given them a word either for the group or the wider church. Indeed, the same claim is sometimes made by people who maintain that

our Lady, or an angel, has given them a message. A person endowed with a genuine charism of discernment might sense whether such messages were inspired by the Lord or not. In the modern charismatic movement, however, the charism of discernment is normally understood in a wider sense, as an ability to assess the authenticity of any inspiration, charismatic or otherwise. If the charism of discernment is understood in this second, wider sense, then it would probably merge into the following form.

Connatural discernment

Secondly, there is what is known technically as connatural discernment. It is rooted in the gifts of wisdom and knowledge mentioned in Isaiah 11:2, and enables some people to have an instinctive sense of what is divinely inspired. St. Thomas wrote in the *Summa Theologiae*: "To judge well about the things of God...through a certain oneness in nature with God is an act of the Spirit's gift of wisdom. Such sympathy or connaturality i.e. an affinity, or quasi-natural rapport with divine things is an effect of the love of charity uniting us to God, so that wisdom's cause is love in the will, even if in essence wisdom is a disposition of mind to judge well. The gift of understanding guides the mind's perceptions, but the gifts of wisdom and knowledge form its judgments." Thomist scholar Garrigou-Legrange has written, by way of explanation, "As the bee or carrier pigeon is directed by instinct, and acts with a wonderful certainty revealing the Intelligence which directs them, just so, says St. Thomas, the spiritual person is inclined to act, not principally through the movement of his own will, but by the instinct of the Holy Spirit." This, it seems to me, is the most common form of discernment among devout Christians. For example, in everyday life, if you know somebody very well, it only takes a micro-second, a syllable of speech, to distinguish his or her voice from that of everyone else who might phone you. It is much the same for people who enjoy a close personal relationship with Jesus. When they receive an inspiration, they can distinguish the voice of the Lord from any other. As a result, they have an intuitive sense of what is good or bad, right or wrong, true or false, Godly or un-Godly.

Isn't this what Jesus promised when he said, "The Spirit will lead you into all truth", Jn 16:13. We can note in passing that this point finds an echo in at last three other New Testament texts. The first says: "As for you, the anointing that you received from God abides in you, and so you do not need anyone to teach you all things", 1 Jn 2:17. The second adds, "I will put my laws in their minds, and write them on their hearts", Heb 8:10. Finally, the third assures us that "What no eye has seen, nor ear heard, nor the human heart conceived.. God has revealed to us through the Spirit; for the Spirit searches everything even the depths of God...(so) we have the mind of Christ", 1 Cor 2:9-10;16.

Pope John Paul II wrote about this kind of inspiration in par. 64 of *Veritatis Splendor*. Although it is a bit difficult to understand at first reading, it is worth quoting at some length. "It is the 'heart' converted to the Lord and to the love of what is good which is really the source of true judgments of conscience. Indeed, in order to 'prove what is the will of God, what is good and acceptable and perfect', Rm 12:2, knowledge of God's law in general is necessary, but it is not sufficient: what is essential is a sort of 'connaturality' between man and the true good. Such a connaturality is rooted in and develops through the virtuous attitudes of the individual himself: prudence and the other cardinal virtues, and even before these the theological virtues of faith, hope and charity. This is the meaning of Christ's saying: "He who does what is true comes into the light", Jn 3:21.

The art of discernment

Thirdly, there is the art of discernment. Instead of relying solely on a charismatic gift or an intuitive ability, this experiential approach is based on a traditional way of assessing religious inspirations. It can be traced back to early Church Fathers such as The Shepherd of Hermas (90 approx), Evagrius Ponticus (346-399) and John Cassian (370-435). How can we judge whether an inspiration comes from God or not? Mindful that Jesus said: "by their fruits you shall know them", Mt 7:16, can we judge by looking at external actions? In other words, if an action is good in itself e.g. doing voluntary work for the homeless, can we presume that the inspiration that prompted such action came from God? We can arrive at an answer by looking at the parable of the Pharisee and tax collector.

It is obvious that the religious official was leading a very good life from an external point of view. He spoke the truth when he said, "I thank you that I am not like other men – robbers, evildoers, adulterers – or even like this tax collector. I fast twice a week and give a tenth of my income." But Jesus wasn't impressed. Despite his good actions, the Pharisee suffered from an off putting dose of inner pride and conceit. The tax collector, on the other hand, led a bad life from the outward point of view. But inwardly, at least he was honest and humble before the Lord. And so, despite his bad actions, Jesus says that he went home in a better spiritual state than the Pharisee. If we cannot base discernment of spirits on external fruits such as good actions, what can we base it on?

Unlike those evangelicals and charismatics who sometimes espouse a dualistic view, the Catholic tradition has always believed that rather than coming from either God or the Evil One, many if not most of our inspirations come from ourselves e.g. our hearts as centres of subjectivity. The heart as Jeremiah 17:9 reminds us, "is devious above all else; it is perverse – who can understand it?" In contemporary language we could say that the unconscious mind, especially its darker side, can exert a large but unacknowledged influence upon our conscious intentions. For example, the person who is inspired to help the homeless, could be motivated by an unconscious feeling of resentment and guilt, or by a desire to appear to be charitable in his own eyes or the eyes of others.

Consolation and desolation of spirit

Over the centuries, spiritual writers like St. Ignatius of Loyola have come to see that if an inspiration is prompted by God, it will be associated with inner consolation, i.e. fruits of the Spirit, such as the joy and peace which are mentioned in Galatians 5:22. When an inspiration has not been prompted by God, it will tend to lead to inner desolation. St. Vincent de Paul has written, that "a mark of illusions and false inspirations is that they are persistent and troublesome and make us uneasy," whereas the ones that come from God "instill themselves gently into our souls and incline us to seek whatever concerns the greater glory of God." Speaking of the difference between consolation and desolation St. Ignatius wrote: "Desolation is the contrary of consolation. Contrary to peace there is conflict; contrary to joy, sadness: contrary to hope in higher things, hope in base things; contrary to heavenly love, earthly love; contrary to tears, dryness; contrary to elevation of mind, wandering of mind to contemptible things."

In his autobiography, Ignatius described how he first noticed this distinction. When he was recovering from a war wound he was aware of two strong desires. The first was evoked when he read lives of Christ and the saints. They filled him with a desire to do great things for God. The second was evoked by the thought of an attractive woman at court. He desired to serve her as her knight. He noticed that while he entertained each of these desires he experienced consolation. However, as soon as he stopped thinking of that lady at court "he was dry and discontented." On the other hand, when he stopped thinking of imitating Christ and the saints, "he remained happy and content." Ignatius went on to tell us: "He began to marvel at the difference and to reflect upon it, realising from experience that some thoughts left him sad and others happy. Little by little he came to recognise the difference between the spirits that influenced him, one from the demon, the other from God."

Be guided by the Spirit

Saint Paul once said: "Live by the Spirit, and you will not gratify the desires of the sinful nature... if you are led by the Spirit, you are not under law", Gal 5:16;18. As was noted in chapter nine, a number of scripture scholars agree that this verse is the key to Christian morality. For instance, in a long book on Paul's teaching on the Spirit, Gordon Fee says that, although the phrase "be guided by the Spirit," occurs only here in the Pauline letters, both the argument in which it occurs and the rest of Pauline theology indicate that this is Paul's basic ethical teaching. When trying to discern the origin of inspirations you will probably find the following words, taken from the writings of St. John Eudes (1601-1670), will be helpful:

1. The spirit of Jesus is a spirit of light, truth, devotion, love, trust, zeal and reverence toward God and the things of God. The spirit of the world is a spirit of error, disbelief, darkness, blindness, mistrust, grumbling, impiety, irreverence and hardness of heart toward God and the things of God.

2. The spirit of Jesus is a spirit of humility, modesty, distrust of self, mortification, self-denial, reliability and firmness among those who live with this spirit. On the contrary, the spirit of the world is a spirit of pride, presumption, disordered self-love, frivolousness and irresponsibility .

3. The spirit of Jesus is a spirit of mercy, charity, patience, gentleness and of unity toward our neighbour. The spirit of the world is a spirit of vengeance, envy, impatience, anger, calumny and division.

4. Finally, the spirit of Jesus is the spirit of God, a holy and divine spirit, a spirit of every type of grace, virtue and blessing. It is a spirit of peace and tranquility, a spirit that only seeks the interests of God and his glory. On the contrary, the spirit of the world is the spirit of Satan. For Satan is the prince and leader of the world. Thus it follows necessarily that the world is animated and governed by his spirit; an earthly, carnal and animal spirit, a spirit of every sort of sin and malediction, a spirit of unrest and anxiety, of storm and tempest, a spirit of devastation, Ps 10:7. It is a spirit that seeks only its own ease, satisfaction and interest.

We all of us have a personal responsibility to discern what spirit is motivating us. The vital question is this, is it the Spirit of God? If it isn't, not only will it obscure the will of God, it will tend to break the bonds of unity upon which the effectiveness of our evangelisation depends. *In Mission of the Redeemer,* Pope John Paul II said in par. 87 that the key to evangelistic spirituality, "is expressed first of all by a life of complete docility to the Spirit. It commits us to being moulded from within by the Spirit, so that we may become ever more like Christ. It is not possible to bear witness to Christ without reflecting his image, which is made alive in us by grace and the power of the Spirit. This docility then commits us to receive the gifts of fortitude and discernment, which are essential elements of missionary spirituality."

Section Four:

Sent

Chapter Nineteen

The New Evangelisation

It is my belief that a profound change is currently taking place in the Catholic Church, one that many clergy and lay people are not yet aware of. It is a striking fact that although the words evangelise and evangelisation were not mentioned even once at Vatican I, they were mentioned 49 times at Vatican II. Ever since then, the Popes, especially Paul VI and John Paul II have repeatedly stressed the need for Catholics to engage in evangelisation. In par 14 of his apostolic exhortation, *On Evangelisation in the Modern World,* Paul VI said: "We wish to confirm once more that the task of evangelising all people constitutes the essential mission of the Church. It is a task and mission which the vast and profound changes of present-day society make all the more urgent. Evangelising is in fact the grace and vocation proper to the Church, her deepest identity. She exists to evangelise." In par. 18, Pope Paul said that evangelisation actually has two sides, personal and collective: "The Church evangelises when she seeks to convert solely through the divine power of the message she proclaims, both the personal and collective consciences of people, the activities in which they engage, and the lives and concrete milieu which are theirs."

Subsequently John Paul II said in his encyclical letter *Mission of the Redeemer* par. 3, "I sense that the moment has come to commit all of the Church's energies to the new evangelisation." It is worth noting that the Holy Father didn't say that the Church should devote some, or many of its resources to a new evangelisation, but rather, ALL of them.

What is the New Evangelisation?

The late Pope John Paul II explained that this evangelisation is not new in content, "The new evangelisation," he said, "begins with the clear and emphatic proclamation of the gospel...it must in no way compromise the distinctiveness and integrity of the Christian faith." In 1991, while commissioning families of the Neo-Catechumenal Way the Holy Father stated: "The task which awaits you—the new evangelisation—demands that you present... the eternal and unchanging content of the heritage of the Christian faith. As you well know it is not a matter of merely passing on a doctrine, but rather of a personal and profound meeting with the Saviour." In a talk given in 2000, now Pope Benedict XVI, went on to explain to catechists in Rome that the New Evangelisation focuses on four key topics, conversion, the kingdom of God, Jesus Christ and eternal life.

Although the Gospel is unchanging, the culture in which it is proclaimed is changing all the time so the Good News has to be inculturated i.e. expressed in a contemporary way that will make sense to the people of our time. In par. 52 of his encyclical *Mission of the Redeemer*, Pope John Paul II said that inculturation,"means the intimate transformation of authentic cultural values, through their integration in Christianity and the insertion of Christianity in the various human cultures." In pars. 58-60 of *The Church in Europe* he spelt out the implications for our respective countries. To do this effectively, John Paul explained, a proclamation is needed that is new in "ardour, methods and forms of expression."

I think it would be true to say that there are two main forms of evangelisation. On the one hand there are the traditional foreign missions which seek to bring the Good News to unbelievers in foreign countries e.g. in Africa or Asia, and on the other hand there is the New Evangelisation which seeks to evangelise people who live in traditionally Christian cultures like Ireland and Britain.

The content of the New Evangelisation
As par. 11 of the *Decree on Ecumenism* points out, in Christianity there is a hierarchy of truths. We refer to the foundation truths of faith as the *kerygma* (in Greek it

means, proclamation, announcement, preaching). C.H. Dodd suggested in the first chapter of his influential book The *Apostolic Preaching and Its Developments,* that the kerygma has six key elements:
1. The Age of Fulfillment has dawned, the 'latter days' foretold by the prophets.
2. This has taken place through the birth, life, ministry, death and resurrection of Jesus Christ
3. By virtue of the resurrection, Jesus has been exalted at the right hand of God as messianic head of the new Israel.
4. The Holy Spirit in the church is the sign of Christ's present power and glory.
5. The messianic age will reach its consummation in the return of Christ.
6. An appeal is made for repentance with the offer of forgiveness, the Holy Spirit, and salvation.

There are a number of kerygmatic statements in the New Testament e.g., Acts 2:14-41; 3:12-4:4; 4:8-12; 5:27-32; 10:34-48; Romans 1:1-4; 1 Timothy 3:16. The challenge for those engaged in the new evangelisation is to express those truths in a way that makes sense in contemporary culture. Once people are established in the liberating experience of salvation we can build upon it by means of catechesis. One of the big mistakes we make in contemporary Christianity is that we presume that, because people are baptised and confirmed, they are already aware of the power of the kerygma. As a result, most of the teaching that is given in church and in school attempts to build on sand. Recognising this, the new evangelisation concentrates, first and foremost, on the proclamation of the kerygma e.g. by means of Alpha courses and Life in the Spirit seminars.

Who is the focus of the New Evangelisation?

The new Evangelisation focuses on the following groups. Firstly, there are practicing Catholics who are sacramentalised but not fully evangelised. As we know, there are many people who, in spite of attending Church on a regular basis, do not seem to have either a personal relationship with Christ or a firm inner conviction that they are justified not by their personal merit but by grace through their faith in Christ's saving death and resurrection, cf. Gal 2:16. Often the faith that Church goers profess on Sunday fails to have a discernible impact on the way in which they live during the week, e.g. in matters of business and sexual ethics.

Nowadays, there is a good deal of talk about the un-churched, i.e. people who are inactive for a long time and only turn up in church for baptisms, deaths and marriages. Speaking about them, Paul VI said in par. 56 of *Evangelisation in the Modern World*, "There are a great numbers of people who have been baptised and, while they have not formally renounced their membership of the church, they are is it were on the fringe of it and do not live according to her teaching." Archbishop Marin of Dublin echoed that point on June 23rd 2008, when setting up the diocesan office for evangelisation, "I have said on a number of occasions that the numbers of those who regularly participate in the Eucharist in our diocese is dropping and many baptised Catholics no longer know Jesus. His message does not touch their lives."

Finally there are unbelievers such as agnostics and atheists as well as members of other faiths such as Jews, Moslems, and Hindus. We are called to evangelise them also. Cardinal Ratzinger, now Pope Benedict XVI, warned in *Lord Jesus*, that Catholics should avoid a false form of political correctness which maintains that all religions are equally valid ways to God. In spite of the fact that non-Christian religions can be means of grace, as par. 16 of the *Dogmatic Constitution on the Church* makes clear, we need to be convinced that what Paul said in 1 Timothy 2:5 is crucially important: "There is one God and one mediator between God and men, the man Jesus Christ."

Motives for evangelising

First and foremost there is the great commission of Jesus in Mark 16:15. We proclaim the coming of the Kingdom of God as Jesus told us to do. As Pope John Paul II said in par. 18 of *Mission of the Redeemer*, "The kingdom of God is not a concept, a doctrine, or a program subject to free interpretation, but it is before all else a person with the face and name of Jesus of Nazareth, the image of the invisible God."

Secondly, we try to share in the ardent zeal of Jesus to save the lost, those who, as a result of un-repented sin, are on the wide road that leads to perdition, cf. Mt 7:13-14. As St. Paul observed in Galatians 5:19-21, "The acts of the sinful nature are obvious: sexual immorality, impurity and debauchery; idolatry and witchcraft; hatred, discord, jealousy, fits of rage, selfish ambition, dissensions, factions and envy; drunkenness, orgies, and the like. I warn you, as I did before, that those who live like this will not inherit the kingdom of God." In 1 Corinthians 6:9-10 he says something similar: "Do not be deceived; neither fornicators nor idolaters nor adulterers nor boy prostitutes nor sodomites nor thieves nor the greedy nor drunkards nor slanderers nor robbers will inherit the Kingdom of God." Those who engage in the New Evangelisation are animated by a heartfelt desire not only to reveal the dangers of sinful living, but also to reveal the unconditional mercy and love of God in such an anointed way that it invites people to admit, and confess their sins, while opening their hearts to God's liberating self communication in the Holy Spirit. As the Lord says in Ezekiel 33:9 "if you warn the wicked to turn from his way, and he does not turn from his way; he shall die in his iniquity, but you will have saved your life."

How shall we evangelise?

This is a huge subject. I will only make six overlapping points here. Firstly we need to share in Christ's heart for the lost. His attitude is well expressed in Matthew 9:36, where we read: "When he saw the crowds, he had compassion for them, because they were harassed and helpless, like sheep without a shepherd." I heard the Rev. Ken Wilson, one of the leaders of the Vineyard fellowship in the U.S. speaking in a very moving way about how he had asked God to enable him to share in his heart for the lost. As a result the Lord gave him a powerful awareness of Christ's thirst on the cross, a thirst not for water but for souls. We need that kind of zeal in order to go searching for the prodigal sons and daughters of our time.

Secondly, we need to realise that a profound reorientation is underway, one that is moving clergy and lay people, alike, away from a maintenance to a missionary model of Church. Not only will it require a fundamental change in our way of thinking, it will also need to find expression in appropriate structural and practical innovations.

Thirdly, I believe that every diocese needs a well resourced office for the New Evangelisation. Every parish needs to have a purpose or mission statement which includes a reference to the new evangelisation. I also believe that parish councils need to have an evangelisation committee which intentionally targets, if needs be with help from the diocesan office, the three different categories of people already mentioned. They can do this for example, by putting on such things as Life in the Spirit Seminars, the different types of Alpha course, Cafe, RCIA, or Cursillo weekends. I think there is a particular need to focus on young adults, many of whom are drifting away from the Church.

Fourthly, we witness to Christ by means of a Christian life

well lived. By bearing silent witness said Pope Paul VI in par. 21 of *Evangelisation in the Modern World* "these Christians will inevitably arouse a spirit of enquiry in those who see their way of life, Why are they like this? Why do they live this way? Why are they among us? Witness of this kind constitutes in itself a proclamation of the good news, silent but strong and effective." This form of evangelisation is dealt with in par. 42 of the *Mission of the Redeemer*, where we read: "The evangelical witness which the world finds most appealing is that of concern for people, and of charity toward the poor, the weak and those who suffer. The complete generosity underlying this attitude and these actions stands in marked contrast to human selfishness. It raises precise questions which lead to God and to the Gospel. A commitment to peace, justice, human rights and human promotion is also a witness to the Gospel when it is a sign of concern for persons and is directed toward integral human development."

Fifthly, all of us as individuals need to develop the courage and skill to do one-to-one evangelisation both within and outside our family circle. As Pope Paul VI said in par. 46 of *Evangelisation in the Modern World*, "side by side with the collective proclamation of the gospel, the other form of evangelisation, the person-to-person one, remains valid and important." It is a matter of seeing openings and knowing how to raise meaning of life topics such as, what do you think happens after death? We need to know and share the core message of Christianity. One way of doing this in a non-preachy way is to share our own testimony. I think that each of us should write and commit to memory a brief account of our religious awakening. It should describe three things, what you were like before the awakening occurred, the religious experience itself, and the effect it had on your life.

Sixthly, in pars. 54-56 of his *The Coming of the New Millennium*, Pope John Paul II pointed out that we can evangelise by means of inter-religious dialogue i.e. a relationship of openness and exchange with other philosophies, cultures and religions. In par 55 of *The Church in Europe* he stated: "As is the case with the overall commitment to the 'new evangelisation', so too proclaiming the Gospel of hope calls for the establishment of a profound and perceptive inter-religious dialogue, particularly with Judaism and with Islam." In par. 56 of *The Coming of the New Millennium* Holy Father explained: "Dialogue, however, cannot be based on religious indifferentism, and we Christians are in duty bound, while engaging in dialogue, to bear clear witness to the hope that is within us, cf. 1 Pt 3:15... As the recent Declaration *Lord Jesus* stressed, this cannot be the subject of a dialogue understood as negotiation, as if we considered it a matter of mere opinion: rather, it is a grace which fills us with joy, a message which we have a duty to proclaim." For example, one could imagine that a Christian could have a fruitful dialogue with either Jews or Moslems about the identity and role of Jesus Christ.

Seventhly, we know that not only did Jesus demonstrate the

truth of what he preached by means of deeds of power such as healing, exorcism and miracle working, he commissioned the apostles and their successors to do the same in his name. Thanks to the revival of the charisms in the contemporary Church, many Christians can manifest the presence of the risen Lord by means of supernatural deeds. Pope Benedict acknowledged this when he wrote, "In the heart of a world adversely affected by rationalistic scepticism, a new experience of the Holy Spirit has come about, amounting to a worldwide renewal movement. What the New Testament describes with reference to the charisms as visible signs of the coming of the Spirit is no longer merely ancient, past history: this history is becoming a burning reality today."

Conclusion

To make the transition described in this chapter is going to require a lot of change, effort and commitment. In par. 49 of *The Church in Europe*, John Paul II wrote, "Europe calls out for credible evangelisers, whose lives, in communion with the Cross and Resurrection of Christ, radiate the beauty of the Gospel. Such evangelisers must be properly trained. Now more than ever a missionary consciousness is needed in all Christians, beginning with Bishops, priests, deacons, consecrated persons, catechists and teachers of religion: "All the baptised, since they are witnesses of Christ, should receive a training appropriate to their circumstances, not only so that their faith does not wither for lack of care in a hostile environment such as the secularist world, but also so that their witness to the Gospel will receive strength and inspiration." The implication of this is that we will need to establish and resource schools of evangelisation. Happily, there are already a number of them in these islands.

Chapter Twenty

Praying Briefly for Others: Some Guidelines

All baptised people can pray in a compassionate way that others might be healed. Such prayer can be made with the laying on of hands, anointing with the oil of gladness, or by means of intercession alone. This is a tentative model to help you remember a few basic stages when it comes to praying in a brief way for people with ailments.

1 Short interview.
While looking the person in the eye ask for his or her first name. Assure the person that all that happens is subject to confidentiality. Ask pertinent questions:
• How are you hurting and in need? It could be physical e.g. arthritis, emotional e.g. depression, or a combination of both.
• How long has it been going on?

- Are you on medication?

2. Diagnosis
Like a good doctor you try to diagnose the root problem. This is usually the result of a combination of graced experience, a knowledge of psychology, and a gift of wisdom which could come in the form of a word of knowledge. Either way one needs to pray for insight.

A. If the presenting problem is psychological or emotional in nature, it is good to try to establish what caused it. For example, many years ago a man told me he could only sleep if the light was on, and someone was with him, usually his wife (Sometimes it was his mother-in-law!). I asked him about his past, in the belief that his problem was due to a forgotten trauma. When we got nowhere I prayed for a word of knowledge. I saw a dead woman laid out in an upstairs room. She looked old enough to be a granny. I asked the man about his grannies. He told me how his mother had made him go into a bedroom to kiss her dead mother. I said, "that is the root problem, you associate bedrooms with death." I prayed for a healing of that memory and he had no problem afterwards.

B. Many physical conditions are what is referred to as the 'presenting problem.' In other words, although the client mentions a physical condition, the true root cause may be psychosomatic in origin. For example, I can remember two daughters bringing their arthritic mother to see me. I discovered that she had suffered from physical ailments all her life. When I talked with them I suspected that the mother was suffering from a spirit of infirmity which was probably rooted in a childhood trauma. I prayed for enlightenment and saw the picture of a dead woman and a child crying. I asked the woman, "did your mother die when you were about 9 or 10?" Before she could answer, her daughters chimed in, "yes she did, and mammy said that she never really recovered from that hurt." So I prayed for healing of that memory and against a spirit of infirmity, in the belief that it was the root of the arthritic problem.

C. One of the things I try to diagnose is whether the person's problem is due, in part at least, to some kind of spiritual oppression which might require a deliverance prayer. For instance, a woman might talk about repeated sex abuse endured in her childhood. Besides wounding her in a psychosexual way, it may have created an opening for oppression by an evil spirit. In a situation like that a simple exorcism is needed. I had to deal with such a case recently.

3. Prayer selection

One needs the wisdom, which the Holy Spirit supplies, to know what kind of prayer would be appropriate in the circumstances. By the way, when in doubt, pray quietly in tongues. There are a number of possibilities:

- If the presenting problem is psychological in nature, then prayer for inner healing is called for.
- If the physical problem is rooted in a hurting memory, prayer for healing of memories may be required.
- If the hurt is associated with unresolved resentment or anger, there is need to lead the person to say a prayer of

unconditional forgiveness and/or thanks in the belief that God allowed the hurt for a reason, to bring a greater blessing from it.
- If there is spiritual oppression involved, deliverance prayer/exorcism may be needed.

4. Prayer engagement

One way or another, one needs to be careful to pray within the measure of faith one has received, cf. Rm 12:3. There are two possibilities, a prayer of command or a prayer of petition. The prayer of command can only be uttered in so far as one is confident that one is praying within the will of God e.g. as a result of a word of knowledge. Over the years I have found that one can say a prayer of command that lies half way between a hesitant and unhesitating faith. For example one might say something like this. "Lord, nothing is impossible to you. In your Name I say to this sickness, yield to the healing power of God at work within you. May the Holy Spirit, the Lord and giver of life hasten to accomplish God's loving and life giving purposes within you. And I thank you Lord, that even now divine grace is at work in this situation. Amen." Notice that such a prayer is non-specific. While affirming in a *general* sense that God is at work in the situation it does not directly address a *particular* illness e.g. cancer, by telling it with thanksgiving to go. The beauty of a prayer like this is twofold. Firstly, it allows one to go to the limit of the measure of faith one currently experiences. Secondly, it disposes the heart to receive a revelation of God's will in this particular situation of ministry. This would authorise the praying person to utter a more specific command with the new measure of expectant faith which has been prompted by God.

Prayer for others does not need to be long drawn out. By and large it is better to pray in twos. This is especially the case when a man or woman is praying for someone of the opposite gender. This guards against unconscious sexual influences being at work. It is sometimes good to ask the client how they think the prayer is going. His or her response might help the person praying to know how best to continue. If you are praying for a physical ailment you might in some circumstances encourage the person to do some action which would enable them to claim their healing, e.g. asking a man with a shoulder problem to try raising his hand higher than usual, in the belief that as he does so, the healing will become established.

If there is any likelihood of people being 'slain in the spirit' it is necessary to have a catcher. Increasingly, scarves or some other kind of covering is made available for women so that due decorum and dignity is preserved.

5. Post Prayer Direction

When the prayer is complete, it is sometimes appropriate to utter a word of direction/encouragement. It can take a number of forms. For example, if the person is on medication for his or her ailment, encourage them not to come off it without the consent of their doctor. Sometimes a condition will require what is referred to as "soaking prayer" i.e. repeated sessions of ministry. Tell the person that if they need more prayer to feel free to ask for it. It is also important to tell the person not to focus on his or her symptoms, e.g. whether they are lessening. Rather, he or she should keep attention on God who is greater than the problem. They can do this by thanking and praising him for whatever grace he is giving them. If the person does experience some kind of healing it is important not to make a premature claim or to exaggerate what has happened. It has been clearly established that in some cases people experience temporary pain relief as a result of the natural placebo effect which causes opiates to be secreted temporarily in the brain. However, if the cessation of pain lasts over three weeks, it is safe enough to testify to a healing. Needless to say, people who pray for others will often continue to pray for their clients following the brief prayer encounters described here.

Chapter Twenty One

Unity and Evangelisation

In the mid nineteen seventies I headed off with Cecil Kerr, a Church of Ireland friend, to an ecumenical Charismatic conference in Malines, Belgium. It was sponsored by Cardinal Leon Joseph Suenens. If my memory services me correctly, the main topic for discussion was the role of Mary in Christianity, was she a sign of unity or division? Representatives from denominations from all over the world were present. Among them was Graham Pulkinham, an Episcopal priest from the Church of the Holy Redeemer in Huston, Texas. That same year his Church had been nominated by *Time* Magazine as the 'best' in the United States. At one point during the conference he was invited by the Cardinal to speak to us about his experiences of Renewal. He described how he had taken over a Church that was dying, and how it was turned around as a result of an outpouring of the Spirit and his gifts. He went on to tell us about the commitment of the parishioners to prayer. I can recall him saying that many of the men used to gather early in the morning to pray before going to work. Then he went on to say something that I will never forget. He stated that there could be no effective evangelisation without unity of mind and heart. Then he opened and read Acts 4:32-36. "All the believers were one in heart and mind. No one claimed that any of his possessions was his own, but they shared everything they had. With great power the apostles continued to testify to the resurrection of the Lord Jesus, and much grace was upon them all. There were no needy persons among them. For from time to time those who owned lands or houses sold them, brought the money from the sales and put it at the apostles' feet, and it was distributed to anyone as he had need."

Afterwards he commented on the passage. He invited us to notice that it was an idealised picture of the New Testament Church. It was mostly about unity of mind and heart which was expressed in a community of goods. But he said that we should notice how verse 33 about evangelisation: "With great power the apostles gave their testimony to the resurrection of the Lord Jesus, and great grace was upon them all," sticks up like a sore thumb in the middle of a passage about unity. Pulkinham observed, "this may not be strictly logical from a literary point of view. But it is absolutely correct from a theological and experiential perspective. Effective evangelisation needs to be rooted in and energised by a united community which is simultaneously the icon of the good news message being preached." I can quite honestly say that Pulkinham's observations on Acts 4:32-36, have influenced me more deeply than anything else I have heard about evangelisation.

Friendship and evangelisation in the New Testament Church

A number of exegetical comments can be made about the verses in Acts 4:32-36. Firstly, the opening one echoes the teaching of the Greeks, Jews and Romans on the nature of friendship. For example, in the 5th century B.C. Pythagoras founded a community of friends. It had four guidelines.

- Friends share in the perfect communion of a single spirit.
- Friends share everything in common.
- Friends are equals, and friendship is an indication of equality.
- A friend is a second self.

A number of exegetes have suggested that St. Luke, who was a Gentile familiar with Greek thought, was consciously and deliberately saying that, thanks to the transforming power of grace, the early Christians fulfilled the ancient ideal of friendship i.e. unity of mind and heart expressed in a community of goods. The friendship between David and Jonathan in 1 Samuel 18:1-5 epitomised this ideal "Jonathan became one spirit with David and loved him as himself (unity of mind and heart)... he swore eternal friendship for him. He took off the robe he was wearing and gave it to David, together with his armour and also his sword and his belt (community of goods)." Although some members of the early Christian church may have been intimate friends, I don't think that Luke was implying that all the members were necessarily sharing their inmost thoughts and feelings with one another. They were one in mind and heart in so far as they were conformed to the mind and heart of Christ.

St. Paul seemed to endorse this interpretation when he said: "Be of the same mind, having the same love, being in full accord and of one mind...Let the same mind be in you that was in Christ", Phil 2:2. In another place he added: "May the God who gives endurance and encouragement give you a spirit of unity among yourselves as you follow Christ Jesus so that with one heart and mouth you may glorify the God and Father of our Lord Jesus Christ", Rm 15:5-6. He also said: "I appeal to you, brothers and sisters, in the name of our Lord Jesus Christ, that all of you agree with one another so that there may be no divisions among you and that you may be perfectly united in mind and thought;" 1 Cor 1:10 and "Finally, all of you, live in harmony with one another; be sympathetic, love as brothers and sisters, be compassionate and humble", 1 Pt 3:8.

In 1977, Ralph Martin spoke the following striking prophecy in Kansas; "Mourn and weep, for the body of my Son is broken. Mourn and weep, for the body of my Son is broken. Come before me with sackcloth and ashes, come before me with tears and mourning, for the body of my Son is broken. I would have made you one new man, but the body of my Son is broken. I would have made you a light on a mountain top, a city glorious and splendorous that all the world would have seen, but the body of my Son is broken. The light is dim. My people are scattered. The body of my Son is broken. Turn from the sins of your fathers. Walk in the ways of my Son. Return to the plan of your Father, return to the purpose of your God. The Body of my Son is broken."

Ecumenism and evangelisation

Evangelisation will only be effective to the extent that it is rooted in Christian unity. That is why Jesus prayed: "may they all be one; even as you, Father, are in me, and I in you, that they also may be in us, so that the world may believe that it is you who sent me", John 17:21. Not only is there a need for unity with our Churches and parishes, we also need as much unity as possible between our Churches. Many years ago I heard that before the collapse of the Soviet Union there was a museum in Moscow devoted to atheism. One section depicted the divisions between the Christian churches and the violence they had caused in many places e.g. in Northern Ireland. What conclusion were people to draw from this? Christianity is a sickness that mistakes itself for a cure. So when missionaries go abroad to spread the Good News, it would not be surprising if the locals said, "we don't want to be infected by your divisive religion. It is not good news, it is bad news."

During the many years I have been involved in the ecumenical movement I have found that two things in particular help to overcome our divisions, namely, humility in relationships, and a willingness to forgive past hurts. Sad to say, I have seen many Catholics and Protestants display an attitude of superiority, conceit and even arrogance in their attitudes to one another. One thing is for sure, they are not the attitudes of Jesus who, "made himself nothing, taking the very nature of a servant", Phil 2:7. Over the years I have found the following text a great help in ecumenical meetings. "Do nothing out of selfish ambition or vain conceit, but in humility *consider others better than yourselves* (my italics)", Phil 2:3. Paul said something similar in another of his letters: "Do not think of yourself more highly than you ought, but rather think of yourself with sober judgment, in accordance with the measure of faith God has given you… *Honour one another above yourselves* (my italics)", Rm 12:3,10. The phrases "in humility consider others better than yourselves" and "honour one another above yourselves," are really striking. They are not about the truths we believe in, but rather about our attitudes to one another. Paul was clearly talking about the need to treat members of other Christian denominations with reverence and respect. Like our Lord we should have a metaphorical towel of humility around our waists as we serve one another with honour. I have found that when, by and large, members of other denominations are treated in this way, they respond in the same way and *visa versa*.

Over the centuries Catholics and Protestants have hurt one-another by what they have said, done and failed to do. The only way of overcoming the wounds, prejudices and resentments of the past is by means of heartfelt forgiveness. I learnt this during the Troubles in Northern Ireland. Let me refer to one memorable example. In 1987 the IRA planted a bomb on the route of a Protestant parade in the town of Enniskillen. Gordon Wilson, a local Methodist, and his daughter Marie were caught in the blast which blew them to the ground and covered them with rubble. In an interview with the BBC, Wilson described his last conversation with his daughter and his feelings towards her killers: "She held my hand tightly, and gripped me as hard as she could. She said, 'Daddy, I love you very much.' Those were her exact words to me, and those were the last words I ever heard her say. But I bear no ill will. I bear no grudge. That sort of talk is not going to bring her back to life. She was a great wee lassie. She loved her profession. She was a pet. She's dead. She's in heaven and we shall meet again. I will pray for these men tonight and every night." No words in more than twenty-five years of violence in Northern Ireland made such a powerful impression on Catholics, both North and South. Indeed when Gordon Wilson was invited to become a non-elected senator in the upper house of the Irish parliament, the Government was acknowledging the esteem in which he was held in the Irish Republic. Until the time of his death he continued to be a credible symbol of reconciliation between Catholics and Protestants, between North and South.

As a result of inter-church humility and mutual forgiveness enormous progress has been made in Northern Ireland and around the world. In the light of their growing love for one another, Catholics and Protestants have discussed the doctrinal differences that have long divided them. Great progress has been made, especially with regard to divisive subjects such as Justification, the Eucharist, Mary, and Church authority. In spite of making considerable progress e.g. the 1998 agreed statement, *Evangelicals and Catholics Together in Ireland* (it is available for download on the Irish Alpha website), there is still a long way to go. But we are encouraged by the words of the psalmist: "How good and pleasant it is when brothers and sisters dwell in unity... *It commands the blessing of the Lord* (my italics)", Ps 133:1,3.

Community and evangelisation

In chapter four above I recounted how many years ago a group I belonged to made a covenant to relate to one another as friends while fasting from any critical or judgmental thoughts or words. This covenant had a remarkable effect. Trust levels grew, praise grew stronger, and the full range of the gifts of the Spirit were released. Around that time we repeatedly asked God to prompt some priest to invite us to conduct a mission in his parish. After about two months, our prayers were answered when the parish priest of a rural area in the mountains of Tyrone invited all sixteen of us to conduct a mini-mission.

The day before we headed off I was apprehensive about the impending visit. I prayed for guidance and was led to look up a certain page in a certain volume of the *Catholic*

Encyclopaedia. It contained a photograph of an ancient manuscript. I asked a colleague, who was good at languages, if it made any sense to him. He said "That is a passage in Hebrew, from the book of Joshua, beginning at chapter one, verse nine. I rushed off to my room, opened my bible and read: "I hereby command you: Be strong and courageous; do not be frightened or dismayed, for the Lord your God is with you wherever you go." When we reached the village the following day, we assembled in the sacristy of the church to pray together. I asked if anyone had received a word of guidance for the day. One of the men answered yes, and read out Joshua 1:9, the very verse I had received in prayer the day before! Then we all confidently headed off in twos to visit homes. Later we had a service of reconciliation, followed by a mass of healing. As a result, many people were reconciled to Christ and a small number were healed of physical and emotional ailments. That mini-mission stands out in my memory because it taught me about the vital link that exists between unity in the community and effective evangelisation.

Conclusion

I am absolutely convinced that unity of mind and heart is essential for all effective evangelisation. As John Paul II said in par. 1 of *Mission of the Redeemer,* "The Council emphasised the Church's "missionary nature," basing it in a dynamic way on the Trinitarian mission itself. The missionary thrust therefore belongs to the very nature of the Christian life, and is also the inspiration behind ecumenism: "that they may all be one...so that the world may believe that you have sent me" (Jn 17:21)." Every group needs to deal with the negative attitudes and feelings that are inimical to unity. The extent to which they are unacknowledged and left unresolved is the extent to which the Holy Spirit will be quenched in the community. That Spirit is the essential influence that animates our evangelisation. As St. Vincent de Paul once said: "Neither philosophy nor theology, nor learned talks influence souls. Jesus Christ must be united with us and we with him. We must work in him and he in us, to speak as he did and with his Spirit." As one hymn puts it so eloquently, *Ubi Caritas, Deus ibi est*, "Where there is love, there is God."

Chapter Twenty Two

Holiness and Evangelisation

Many years ago I was asked to bring Cardinal Owen McCann of Cape Town, South Africa to visit Cardinal Thomas O' Fee in Armagh, Northern Ireland. On the way back, I asked the prelate if he had attended the Second Vatican Council. He told me, in no uncertain terms, that indeed he had. Then I asked him what had impressed him most about the council. Without hesitation, he replied, "Fr. Collins the thing that impressed me most about the Council was the universal call to holiness. It is addressed not only to priests and religious, it is also addressed to the laity in virtue of their baptismal incorporation into Christ." Then he added in an almost prophetic manner, "If you ever write books," - I had no thought of writing at the time - "remember what I have shared with you." When I did finally set pen to paper, a few years later, I recalled the Cardinal's words. More recently, when praying I seemed to receive a prophetic word which went as follows:

"I am the Lord your God the holy one. My people, do not compromise with sin. If there is mortal sin in your life, do not deny or excuse it. Repent, receive my forgiveness, avoid the first stirrings of temptation and believe that I will deliver you from the web of evil that holds you captive. If there is venial sin in your life, do not tolerate it. Be aware that secret and un-repented sin in the lives of those who believe in me is the greatest single obstacle to the work of my Spirit.

"I want you to be holy, I want you to turn away from the ways of the world. I call on you to root out your sins, great and small alike. Be assured that I will not only enlighten your heart to know your sins I will enable you to turn away from them by a great and liberating outpouring of my grace. Be holy as I am holy. There is no substitute for this holiness. There is no plan, effort or activity, no matter how well intentioned, which will accomplish my purposes if you are not holy like Me. When your heart is cleansed, my Spirit will pray ardently within you, it will guide you in ways you have not known, it will empower and protect you from the deceptions of the evil one. It will fill you with my joy.

"I weep for the world and my Church. There are many, who because of their great and repeated sins, are travelling the wide road that leads to perdition. Call them to repentance, before it is too late, so that they may come back to me. I promise you that many of them will heed your words when they see my holiness shining forth in your lives. My people, the time of breach-mending is at hand. I will enable you to re-build the walls of Jerusalem. I am about to accomplish a great work of restoration, but woe to those who do not heed my voice"

As a result of these and other influences I have often pondered the question, what exactly is holiness? To cut a longer story short I came up with a succinct three point description. Holiness is a matter of being filled, guided and empowered by the Spirit of God, cf. Eph 5:18; Gal 5:18; 5:16.

The holiness of Jesus

Needless to say Jesus is the archetypal model of holiness. As God he was holy from the moment of his conception, but as man he seemed to mature in holiness. As St. Luke testified, "And Jesus increased in wisdom, in stature and in favour with God and people", Lk 2:52. One of the decisive moments in his spiritual growth occurred when he was baptised in the Jordan. It strikes me that this mystical experience had three main effects. First, Jesus knew, in a conscious and vivid way that he was loved by his Father. Secondly, in the light of his experience of the infinite love of God Jesus was confirmed in his knowledge that he was the promised messiah, not the messiah of popular expectation, but rather the suffering servant (see Isaiah 53:3). Thirdly, Jesus was aware of his mission. He declared: "The Spirit of the Lord is on me, because he has anointed me to preach good news to the poor", Luke 4:18. As the evangeliser of the poor he was to show to others, especially those who were "sad and dejected like sheep without a shepherd", Mt 9:36, the unconditional and unrestricted love that God was showering on him. God wanted all his words and actions to be rooted in that love, to express that love and to foster that same love among those who believed in him.

From the moment that Jesus went into the wilderness, to be tested, he was led by the spirit, cf. Lk 4:1. That is one of the reasons he spent so much time in prayer. He wanted to seek the will of his Father. Because he was sinless, there was no attachment or impediment which compromised his ability to discern the purposes of God. As he testified, "I have not spoken on my own accord, but the Father who sent me, commanded me what to say and what to speak", Jn 12:49 & 14:31. Later the letter to the Hebrews says that Jesus exemplified the meaning of the verse which says, "I have come to do your will", Heb 10:7.

Jesus was empowered by the Spirit to carry out the nuances of the mission allocated to him by the Father. St. Peter was able to say of him: "You know what has happened throughout Judea, beginning in Galilee after the baptism that John preached - how God anointed Jesus of Nazareth with the Holy Spirit and power, and how he went around doing good and healing all who were under the power of the devil, because God was with him", Acts 10:37-38. It is a striking fact that Jesus demonstrated the truth of the liberating love he proclaimed, not only by the way he related to people and his works of mercy but also by deeds of power.

Filled, guided and empowered by the Spirit

Contemporary Christians have the vocation of being Christ in the world of today. Like their Saviour, they need to be filled, guided and empowered by the Spirit. While it is true that we receive the Holy Spirit in a sacramental way in baptism/confirmation, it needs to be manifested at a conscious level as a result of a religious awakening through baptism in the Holy Spirit. It reveals the length and breadth, the height and depth of the love of Christ which surpasses understanding, and which fills the person with the fullness of God, cf. Eph 3:18-19. This is not a one off event, but the decisive initiation of a life-long process. St. Thomas Aquinas has pointed out that Christians can experience repeated in-fillings of the Spirit. For more on this see chapter eight.

Like Jesus, Christians need to be guided by the Spirit (for more on this see chapter ten). This is the key to Christian ethics. If they truly desire to discover God's will, they can only receive inspired insight if their lives are moulded by the values and beliefs of Jesus. In Ephesians 4:23-24 we read: "be made new in the attitude of your minds; and to put on the new self, created to be like God in true righteousness and holiness." In Romans 12:2 Paul adds: "Do not conform any longer to the pattern of this world, but be transformed by the renewing of your mind. Then you will be able to test and approve what God's will is-- his good, pleasing and perfect will." Paul would have been familiar with the Greco-Roman practice of making statues by pouring molten metal into moulds so that it would assume their shapes. Analogously, Paul was saying to the people, don't let yourselves to be moulded by the values and beliefs of the pagan world.

Like Jesus, our activities have to be empowered by the Spirit. This means that the true evangelist is a humble person, one who in poverty of spirit acknowledges his or her complete dependence on God. Without him we can do nothing, cf. Jn 15:5, but with God's help all things are possible, cf. Mk 9:23. This will only happen if evangelists act in conformity with the will of God. As the psalmist warns, "unless the Lord build the house in vain do the labourers build", Ps 127:1. Pope Paul VI made the same point in par. 75 of *Evangelii Nuntiandi:* "Techniques of evangelisation are good, but even the most advanced ones could not replace the gentle action of the Spirit. The most perfect preparation of the evangeliser has no effect without the Holy Spirit. Without the Holy Spirit the most convincing dialectic has no power over the heart of man. Without Him the most highly developed schemas resting on a sociological or psychological basis are quickly seen to be quite valueless." Needless to say, the Spirit only acts in accord with the divine will.

Conclusion

If my understanding of holiness is correct, we could safely say that, normally, evangelisation will be effective to the extent that the evangelist is holy. As Pope John Paul II said in par. 30 0f *The Coming of the New Millennium*, "I have no hesitation in saying that all pastoral initiatives must be set in relation to holiness." However, it must be said that the Lord can occasionally use sinful people, in spite of their lack of openness to the Spirit, as instruments of his purposes. The notion of the objective efficacy of the sacraments *ex opere operato* (Trent, Sess. VII, can.6, 8) apart from the holiness of the minister, is taught by the Church. St. Thomas Aquinas and Pope Benedict XIV both taught that the Charisms, the *gratis data*, (i.e. in 1 Corinthians 12:8-10) are not necessarily signs that the person exercising them is in the state of grace, however, they can be instrumental in helping others to grow in sanctifying grace.

Chapter Twenty Three
Person to Person Evangelisation

Although the task of preaching the gospel is the responsibility of every baptised person, scripture makes it clear that this task is often entrusted in a special way to gifted individuals such as outstanding preachers and teachers (see Ephesians 4:11). However, we are all of us called to engage in one-to-one evangelisation. Pope Paul VI wrote in par. 46 of *Evangelisation in the Modern World*, "side by side with the collective proclamation of the Gospel, the other form of transmission, the person-to-person one, remains valid and important." In this chapter I want to look at the story of Philip and the Ethiopian in Acts 8: 26-36 because we can all learn from it. Philip was a deacon, and his preaching in Samaria had been accompanied by "miraculous signs", Acts 8:6. I believe that Luke's account of how he led the court official to faith provides us with a seven point template of how to engage in effective one-to-one evangelisation.

1. Guidance

The first thing that Philip's ministry teaches us is that evangelisation has to be led by the Spirit rather than by mere rational planning or a cheerless sense of duty. We are told that: "an angel of the Lord said to Philip, "Go south to the road, the desert road, that goes down from Jerusalem to Gaza", Acts 8:26. In Greek the word for angel literally means messenger. It is possible that Philip received a prophetic word of guidance, either from another member of the community (see Hebrews 13:2) or in a time of personal prayer. As I have mentioned in chapter fourteen, St. Thomas believed that angels were instrumental in the exercise of all the spiritual gifts. One way or the other, Philip knew that "Unless the Lord builds the house, in vain do the labourers build", Ps 127:1.

2. Faith

To travel down the desert road didn't make much sense, from a rational point of view, because it was the place where Philip was least likely to meet anyone. But when he listened to the voice of God he chose to walk by faith and not by sight. In doing so, he carried out the advice of Proverbs 3:5: "Trust in the Lord with all your heart, and lean not on your understanding," and Psalm 37:5 "Trust in the Lord with all your heart, commit your life to him, and he will act."

3. Providence

As Philip walked down the road he saw a distinguished Ethiopian. Scripture scholars say that the word Ethiopian probably refers to the fact that he was black rather than to the country of his origin. In all likelihood he was probably from the upper Sudan or Egypt. In any case, Philip received guidance a second time when the Spirit said to him, "Go over to this chariot and join it," Acts 8:29. Clearly, this was a divinely ordained encounter, an example of how *chronos*, i.e. secular time, suddenly became *kairos* i.e. a sacred moment when the grace of the Lord is manifested in an efficacious way.

4. Attention

Just as Jesus had paid undivided attention to the woman at the well of Samaria, Philip paid empathic attention to the stranger. Straight away he noticed that he had servants and was dressed in fine clothes which indicated that he was a person of power, influence, and wealth. But it was also fairly obvious from his hairless face and high pitched voice that he had been cruelly castrated, probably in his youth. So despite all indications to the contrary, not only was he a lonely man who was unable to marry or have a family, he was also poor in spirit, an outsider who was familiar with injustice and humiliation. He was reading Isaiah 53:7-8 when Philip encountered him. So he asked the official whether he understood the passage. He replied, "How can I unless someone guides me", Acts 8:31.

5. Witnessing

Philip responded to the eunuch's query by telling him that Isaiah had been talking about the suffering servant. Then beginning with Moses and going through all the prophets, he interpreted to him all the things in the scriptures about the Christ (see Luke 24:27). No doubt he told him about the saving death and resurrection of Jesus and how he was willing to pour out his Spirit of merciful love on all who believed in him. It is quite possible that Philip backed up what he said with his own personal testimony. As a result, the eunuch could see that Jesus had completely identified with his own suffering and shame. Like him, Jesus had suffered injustice and had died in his prime without children. This was his moment of revelation. He began to experience the compassion and closeness of the humiliated Christ.

6. Ministry

As soon as Philip stopped speaking, the eunuch asked if he could be baptised. Some early manuscripts say that Philip responded, "if you believe with all your heart, you may. And he said in reply, 'I believe that Jesus Christ is the Son of God", Acts 8:3). As Paul made clear in Romans 10:9 "if you confess with your mouth, 'Jesus is Lord', and believe in your heart that God raised him from the dead, you will be saved." Providentially, there was water nearby. Having heard the eunuch's profession of faith, Philip baptised him there and then.

7. Aftermath

When this wonderful event came to fruition, Philip disappeared, in a way that is reminiscent of the way Jesus disappeared following the breaking of bread in Emmaus (see Lk 24:31). Like any good evangelist Philip continued to spread the good news from Azotus to Cesarea. In Acts 21:8-9 we are told that some time later he was living in Caesarea with his four unmarried daughters who had the gift of prophecy. As for the court official, he went on his way rejoicing. Even though he still had many miles to travel, he had already reached his spiritual destination. Presumably, when he returned to court he evangelised by testifying to the way in which he had committed his life to Christ.

Implications

The story in Acts teaches contemporary evangelisers that:
- Like Philip they need to be people of prayer who are "guided by the Spirit", Eph 5:18.
- They will sometimes have to crucify their sense of rational prudence in order to step out in faith by becoming, "fools for Christ's sake", 1 Cor 4:10.
- Today's evangelists need to be in tune with the nuances of divine providence and to recognise *kairos* moments.
- Instead of following their own agenda, Christian evangelists need to tune in to the religious desires of the people they minister to.
- Then and only then, they witness in an appropriate way to the Good News, sometimes illustrating what they say with their personal testimonies.
- When the listener responds with faith, evangelisers should pray for the other person with expectant faith, believing that God's power will

be at work, cf. Phil 2:13.
- Afterwards, both the evangelisers and the evangelised seek to fulfil the great commission by continuing to spread the good news by means of one-to-one contact.

A Testimony

Some time ago, Paddy Monaghan, who runs Alpha in Ireland, and myself went to a parish cells conference in Milan. We shared a room and began and ended each day with some spontaneous prayers. On our last morning in the city I told my companion that the Lord had given me a word of knowledge about meeting a man later that day who we would evangelise together. Shortly afterwards we headed for the airport and when we got there we went to the cafeteria for a bite to eat.

There was a man with a beard sitting opposite me. He had a number of magazines in front of him. When I noticed that one of them was about motorbikes I asked him if he had one at home. That led to a freewheeling conversation that went from bikes to clocks to computers to the influence of spirituality on health. At that point our chat took a more serious turn. It was clear that while the American was interested in spirituality in a notional way, he didn't seem committed to either God or any Church. At one point he said he had been brought up in the Bible Belt and had been put off by pushy fundamentalist preachers. From what he said I had a suspicion that he himself was an ex-Catholic. Well into the conversation my companion, who had remained uncharacteristically silent up to this point, asked the stranger whether he was a believer. He said that, while he had been raised in a Christian family he wasn't practicing. Paddy then spoke to him about Christ and offered him a pamphlet about the Da Vinci Code, because that particular book had been mentioned in the course of our conversation. Then Paddy surprised me when he encouraged the man to attend an Alpha course in the U.S. and offered him literature to do with the subject. Then he went on to ask him if he would like to be prayed with. To my surprise the American said, a little reluctantly it must be said, that he would. So right there in the crowded cafeteria Paddy said a quiet prayer for the stranger, asking that the Lord would reveal himself to him in a new way. When we parted company I had a conviction that the Lord had fulfilled the word of knowledge he had given me that morning. We had met a man who we were able to evangelise together. Although I didn't know what the final outcome would be, I was confident that the Lord would enable the seed we had planted to bear fruit in the future, perhaps with the help of others. As Paul said: "I planted, Apollos watered, but God gave the growth", 1 Cor 3:6.

That incident taught me a lot about one-to-one evangelisation. When I reflected on it afterwards I could see that even though I'm willing to talk about spiritual issues with other people, I have a typically middle class reluctance to intrude upon the person's privacy by going beyond generalised discussion to talk directly about Jesus as the Way the Truth and the Life. I learned from Paddy that, like Philip, I should take the opportunity when it spontaneously arises, of speaking about Jesus. I also learned the importance of offering to pray with the person in a spirit of expectant faith, that he or she might receive the blessing they most need at the time.

Conclusion

I suspect that one-to-one evangelisation could prove to be the most important in the future. Before concluding, here are just a few of the many possible practical suggestions about how a person might engage in this kind of witness.

1. Prepare a short written version of your personal testimony. Although it is about you, it should focus on how the Lord came into your life and what he has done for you. It could have three main sections: a) Life before your spiritual awakening. b) The spiritual awakening itself. c) Life after the spiritual awakening. Share your faith story with a Christian friend and listen in a non defensive way to his or her feedback. Think of modifying your testimony in the light of what the person has said.

2. Think about how you might initiate spiritual conversations. There are three ways at least of doing this: direct, indirect, and invitational:

• Typically, the direct method takes the form of a question or statement e.g. "Did you ever think about what happens after we die?" "Did you know that on average people who are truly religious are happier and live 7 years longer than people who are not?"

- The indirect method latches on to some topic that has come up in conversation and relates it to a spiritual topic, e.g. the person is talking about the difficulty of dieting or giving up smoking. That would leave the door open to saying something about 12 step programmes and the need for reliance on the Higher Power, namely God, which is closely related to Paul's notion that God's power is made perfect in our weakness. You could think of relatives, colleagues and friends that you would like to evangelise. Could you prepare transition topics, going from what they are interested in to something spiritual?
- The invitational method is used when you invite a colleague or friend to a Christian event you are intending to attend, e.g. a lecture, an Alpha Course, a Christian concert, etc.

A lot more could be said about ways and means of engaging in person to person evangelisation. With God's help I will tackle it in a book I hope to write soon on evangelisation.

Chapter Twenty Four

Worship as a Means of Evangelisation

Recently I had cause to read a book about the Apostolic Fathers. They were the teachers of the Christian faith in the years between around 80 and 150 A.D. Two things struck me in their writings. Firstly, they rarely quoted from New Testament texts, because they were not yet available to the Fathers. Secondly, it is surprising to find that they do not talk very much about the gifts of the Spirit or evangelisation. What is striking is the fact that the Christians witnessed to their faith by means of their community gatherings and the way in which their members resisted the pagan life styles of many of their contemporaries. If pagans attended their meetings they often sensed that the risen Lord was present among the worshippers. Speaking of a pagan's reaction Paul said in 1 Corinthians 14:24-25, "he will be convinced by all that he is a sinner and will be judged by all, and the secrets of his heart will be laid bare. So he will fall down and worship God, exclaiming, "God is really among you!" I'm convinced that charismatic prayer meetings are places where visitors can be evangelised. This can come about as a result of such things as testimonies, teaching, the exercise of the gifts and above all else by praise and worship.

We all had to read sonnets at school. They are poems which express a single idea in fourteen lines. So the rules are strict, but in the hands of a master like William Shakespeare or George Herbert, the poet finds in the form, not bonds but wings. A prayer meeting is similar. It has an identifiable structure and dynamics like a sonnet, within which the leader and participants can express the ever fresh inspirations of the Holy Spirit. So, ideally, good order and spontaneity go hand in hand. Order without spontaneity is lifeless, and spontaneity without order is chaotic. In this chapter, I will examine the importance of worship in prayer meetings. My description is not intended to be a rigid blueprint but rather a resource to help prayer group leaders and participants alike to be more thoughtful about the nature and planning of prayer meetings.

Petition for ourselves and intercession for others is the fundamental form of Christian prayer. It expresses our absolute dependence on God for existence, life, talents, gifts, and graces. The prayer of appreciation including thanks, praise, and adoration is rooted in a sense of gratitude for all that the Lord has given us. It is like a bridge that enables us to cross over from the visible to the invisible, the natural to the supernatural, from this world into the presence of the living God. Praise is a keystone in that bridge, flanked on the one side by thanksgiving, and on the other by worship. We will look at each form of prayer in turn.

Thanksgiving

The word to 'thank' in English is taken from the Old English *thone* which is a cognate with the German *dank*, meaning 'to think', literally, 'to be mindful, to be aware of'. Appreciation as thanksgiving means that one is mindful and grateful for the gifts of God. The prayer segment of the meeting will often begin with either an invocation of the Spirit, or an act of contrition, or with both. Then prayer of appreciation should usually begin with thanksgiving i.e. concentrating with gratitude on the gifts of God. Like the leper who came back to thank Jesus for his healing, we thank God for the graces and blessings we have received. It is good for the prayer group leader to encourage those present to witness to God's goodness to them in the recent past, thereby providing people with good reasons for thanking God. They can respond in:

- Spontaneous words of thanksgiving
- A chorus of a hymn that expresses thanksgiving. It can be repeated after each testimony.
- Or a full hymn/s of thanksgiving.

Praise

The word 'praise' in English is derived from the Latin *pretiare* to prize, which is derived from *pretium* meaning price. Appreciation as praise acknowledges the value of the God of the gifts. The focus shifts from the gifts of God to the God of the gifts. The leader should give some reasons for doing so, by indicating how it could be done in practical ways, while and inviting the people to raise their minds, hearts and voices to the Lord. The people present can contribute in different ways.

- Quoting a suitable reading from the scriptures e.g. part of a psalm of praise such as Psalm 92:1-2. "It is good to praise the Lord and make music to your name, O Most High, to proclaim your love in the morning and your faithfulness at night."
- Use gifts of prophecy, visions or an inspired scripture text. For example, a number of years ago I attended a meeting in Belfast. The praise was fairly pathetic. Then a woman saw an image of birds sitting on a wall. Although they had wings they never seemed to fly. Then the Lord said to her: "Unless the birds use the wings of praise, I will not be able to bear them up on the wind of my Spirit." As soon as they made the decision to praise, the Lord did the rest, until they were lifting the roof with anointed praises.
- Praise hymns can also be used. If those who are in charge of the music have a menu of thanking, praising and worshipping hymns made out, they will be able to find an appropriate praise hymn quickly. If people want to nominate appropriate hymns it is good to say why they want them sung, e.g. by quoting a meaningful line. We

should praise God intelligently, thereby avoiding a rather mindless sing-song approach. Incidentally, groups need to keep on introducing new praise hymns. Otherwise the golden oldies will grow stale through over use.
- Actions can be used judiciously to accompany songs. There are many examples such as "Isn't the love of Jesus simply wonderful," "Father Abraham" and "His banner over me is love."
- Praying and singing in tongues also has an important role to play. When we are praising in English, even the most articulate people quickly run out of things to say even though they still want to praise. That is where the gift of praying and singing in tongues can be so helpful. Although the mind and imagination are at rest the heart and lips can continue to praise the Lord. Thus tongues is a contemplative, pre-rational, non-symbolic form of prayer, which enables the God within to pray to the God beyond.
- As the bible indicates on many occasions, praise should be loud and long. Sirach 43:29-33 says: "Where shall we find strength to praise him? For he is greater than all his works....When you praise the Lord, *exalt him as much as you can*; for he will surpass even that. When you exalt him, *put forth all your strength*, and *do not grow weary*, for you cannot praise him enough. Who has seen him and who can describe him? Or who can extol him as he is?"

In the Old and New Testaments there is the notion of the war cry of praise. It anticipated the victory God was going to bring about. It was intended to strike terror into their enemies, while expressing unshakable confidence in God's help. There is a good example in 2 Chronicles 20. King Jehosophat received news that his kingdom was about to be attacked by three formidable armies. From a military point of view the position looked hopeless. Not surprisingly the king was filled with fear and anxiety. But instead of wrestling with the problem, he nestled by faith in the Lord by means of prayer and fasting. Having poured out his heart to the Lord, Jehosophat waited for a divine response. It came through one of his priests who spoke a word of prophecy. "Your majesty," he said, "and all you people of Judah and Jerusalem, the Lord says you must not be discouraged or afraid to face this large army. The battle depends on God and not on you." 2 Chron 20:15.

We are told that: "early in the morning ....As the army set out, Jehoshaphat stood and said, "Listen to me, Judah and people of Jerusalem! Have faith in the Lord your God and you will be upheld; have faith in his prophets and you will be successful." After consulting the people, Jehoshaphat appointed men to sing to the Lord and to praise him for the splendor of his holiness as they went out at the head of the army, saying: "Give thanks to the Lord, for his love endures forever." In other words, the priests and musicians led the soldiers in shouting war cries as they marched into battle. The scriptures tell us what happened next: "As they began to sing and praise, the Lord set ambushes against the men of Ammon and Moab and Mount Seir who were invading Judah, and they were defeated.", 2 Chr 20:20-22. As the Lord says in Psalm 46:10: "Be still, and know that I am God; I will be exalted among the nations, I will be exalted in the earth."

Late in the Old Testament we find that when the chosen people had settled down in Palestine there were fewer wars. But they remembered the battle cry of victory. They modified it for use in their temple worship. It became the "festal shout" that is sometimes mentioned in the psalms. For example, Psalm 89:15 sums up the biblical attitude when it declares: "Blessed are the people who know the *festal shout*." There are a number of examples of the festal shout in the Old and New Testaments. The three young men praised God in the fiery furnace. Instead of being burnt they were set free, cf. Dan 3:24. Jonah praised God in the belly of the whale. Instead of being lost at sea he was coughed up on the shore, cf. Jonah 2:9-10. On Palm Sunday, the praises of the people constituted a festal shout that anticipated the resurrection of Jesus. As he said on that occasion, if the people didn't utter the festal shout "the stones will cry out" Lk 19:40. A week later, having expressed his sense of spiritual desolation on the cross Jesus went on to recite the rest of Psalm 22 in his heart. Among other things it says in verse 22: "I will declare your name to my brothers and sisters; in the congregation I will praise you." When he *cried* out "Into your hands I commit my spirit" Jesus was uttering his festal shout of victory, which anticipated his triumph over Satan, Sin, and death.

My personal conviction about the importance of the festal shout of praise was nurtured during the troubles in Northern Ireland. Because ecumenically minded Christians seemed to face impossible odds we had to rely on God. For example an inter-faith conference was held in Belfast during the general strike of 1977. There was the threat of violence in the streets and of power failures. Nevertheless, over a thousand Protestants and Catholics gathered in Church House in the centre of the city for a 'Festival of Praise.' It was a remarkable experience. There was an outburst of strong, sustained praise such as I had never heard before. God's anointing fell upon us and we were graced with the festal shout, the kind that anticipates in praise the liberating action of God. In a prophecy the Lord called upon us to be united as his army. "The work and the weapons are one," the Lord said, "they are praise."

Worship

The word 'worship' in English is derived from the Old English *weorth*, meaning 'worth.' Appreciation as worship is a heartfelt awareness of the glory of the Lord. Psalm 95:6 shows how the prayer of appreciation as thanksgiving and praise reaches its point of highest intensity in the form of worship. "Come, let us bow down in *worship*, let us kneel before the Lord our Maker." Worship is commonly expressed in bodily gestures such as the ones described by the psalmist with prostrations, raising of arms, clapping etc. Whereas the members of the meeting are active in thanking and praising God they are more passive in worship. As Psalm 22:3 says: "Yet thou art holy, enthroned on the praises of Israel." As we concentrate on the Lord by means of thanksgiving and praise, the Lord reveals himself to those who are praying. There can be an anointing when the Lord's presence and glory are palpably present. It is then that the people are moved to a deeper type of praise in the form of worship, an awed, quieter acknowledgement of the inestimable worth of God whose majesty exceeds the narrow bounds of our human understanding. Appropriate worship hymns need to be sung at this time. They may melt into either a gentle singing in tongues or into silent adoration. It is at moments like this that the Lord may inspire someone to speak an inspired word to the meeting, either in the form of a prophecy, reading, or word of knowledge. In many groups the prayer of appreciation is followed by a short time of petitions and intercessions.

Conclusion

Finally, I firmly believe that those charged with the responsibility of leading worship should prepare by means of prayer, consultation with others, and thoughtful planning. In this way the worship leader can carry out his or her task with the assurance that God helps those who help themselves. One doesn't have to stick rigidly to the plan. It is a bit like jazz. There is a framework, but one improvises within it as the Spirit leads. I'm convinced that God-centered worship is a powerful means of evangelisation for all who participate in it.

Chapter Twenty Five

Witness to Uncompromising Discipleship

When I was in the seminary about 40 years ago, Gordon Zahn's book, *In Solitary Witness: the Life and Death of Franz Jagerstatter*, was read during the meal times; It made a deep and lasting impression on me. It was about a Catholic peasant from Austria. He was born out of wedlock in 1907, a few miles from Hitler's birth place. Following a rowdy youth, when he fathered a daughter outside wedlock, he had a religious awakening at the age of 27. Two years later he married and had three daughters. Although he was poorly educated, he began to read the Scriptures and spiritual books. He joined the Third Order of St. Francis and occasionally acted as· sacristan in his local church. Around this time he commented in a personal way to his wife: "I can say from my own experience how painful life often is when one lives as a halfway Christian; it is more like vegetating than living."

The two ways

How did Jagerstatter turn his life around? We get a clue from a letter he wrote in 1936 to his godchild Franz Huber who was about 15 or 16 years of age. He warned him about the danger of binge drinking and irresponsible sexual behaviour such as masturbation and fornication. He says that many people, including those who attend Church every Sunday, excuse such behaviour by saying such things as, "whatever nature demands of people can certainly not be sinful." He also says that young people are often slow to resist sexual sin because they fear the taunts of their peers who might say that they were impotent or unable to get a sexual partner.

Speaking of temptation against the sixth commandment he said to his godson: "Should it be that temptation is ever so strong that you feel you must give in to sin, give some thought to eternity. For it often happens that a man risks his temporal and eternal happiness for a few seconds of pleasure. No one can know whether he will ever again have an opportunity to confess or if God will give him the grace to repent of his sin." There seems to have been a strongly autobiographical aspect to what Jagerstatter said. It sounds as if it was this awareness of the long term implications of sin which helped him to repent. Even if it was a case of imperfect contrition at first, it is quite evident that as his spiritual life matured his motivation changed. A time came when he wanted to avoid sin simply because it grieved the Spirit of God within him. He told his godson what he himself had already discovered, "even the most courageous Christians can and will fall, but they will not lie for long in the filth of sin. Instead they will pull themselves together and draw strength from the sacraments of Penance and Holy Communion and strive to their goal." When temptation seemed overwhelming he said, presumably on the basis of personal experience, "let us remember that God burdens none of us with a heavier cross than he can bear." This dimension of Jagerstatter's life is important. It was because he had already learned to die to selfishness and the influence of public opinion, through graced obedience to the word and will of God, that he was able to cope with the moral challenges posed by the Nazi invasion of his country.

Render to God what belongs to God

The Nazis annexed Austria in 1938. As a result of a revelatory dream Franz was convinced that the regime was evil. He referred to national socialism as a shiny train which was leading its many passengers to hell. He was right. The Fuhrer had stated: "I freed Germany from the stupid and degrading fallacies of conscience and morality." In these demonic words he boasted of liberating his country from obedience to God. If proof were needed, Jagerstatter heard subsequently in 1941 how the Nazis were mistreating people who had mental handicaps. Even so, he was the only person in his village to vote against the Anschluss, the political union of Nazi Germany and Austria. He did this despite the fact that his wife Franziska wanted him to go along with everyone else in case he might jeopardise the family's safety. He was so opposed to the regime that he even turned down money to which he was entitled through a Nazi family assistance program. When a storm destroyed the crops in his region, he would not take the emergency aid offered by the authorities.

Like many others, Franz was enlisted into the army. At first he thought it might be OK because he would be obeying the secular authorities and opposing communism. However, soon afterward he refused to fight on the basis that Hitler was conducting an unjust war. His offer to serve in the medical corps was turned down. As a result, he was imprisoned in Linz where he experienced a brief crisis of faith. Many people, including his relatives, parish priest and bishop tried to prevail upon him to change his mind. Instinctively he knew, as Cardinal Newman had said: "Conscience is the original Vicar of Christ." He stated at the time: "Again and again they try to trouble my conscience over my wife and children. Is an action any better because one is married and has children? Is it better or worse because thousands of other Catholics are doing the same?... Everyone tells me, of course, that I should not do what I am doing because of the danger of death. I believe it is better to sacrifice one's life right away than to place oneself in the grave danger of committing sin and then dying." Surely, that moving statement, illustrates exactly what Jesus said about the demands of uncompromising discipleship.

The martyrdom of Franz Jagerstatter

As a result of his objection to fighting in an unjust war, Jagerstatter was tried by a military court and sentenced to death. He was sent to a prison in Berlin. There he was able to receive Holy Communion occasionally; and was encouraged when he heard about the heroic witness of Franz Reinisch, a Pallottine priest, who had already been executed as a conscientious objector. While in prison Jagerstatter wrote: "Just as the man who thinks only of this world does everything possible to make life here easier and better, so must we, too, who believe in the eternal Kingdom, risk everything to receive a great reward there." In his last letter to his wife he said, "Dearest wife and mother! It was not possible for me to free you from the pain that you must suffer now on my account. How hard it must have been for our dear Saviour when, through his sufferings and death, he had to prepare such a great sorrow for his mother." On the day of his execution, Fr. Jochmann, the prison chaplain, spent some time with Jagerstatter. He reported that the prisoner was calm and uncomplaining. He refused any religious material, even a New Testament, saying, "I am completely bound in inner union with the Lord, and any reading would only interrupt my communication with my God." At 4 p.m. that day; Aug. 9, 1943, Franz Jagerstatter was beheaded and later cremated. Afterward Fr. Jochmann told some nuns, "The military beheaded a great man today. He lived as a saint and has died a hero. I feel with certainty that this simple man is the only saint that I have ever met in my lifetime."

Beatification

Now some 64 years later, Fr. Jochmann's impression has been confirmed by Pope Benedict XVI. In June 2007 he declared that Franz Jagerstatter was a martyr for the faith. On the 26th of October 2007 he was beatified in Linz Cathedral by the head of the Vatican's Congregation for the Causes of Saints in the presence of 27 cardinals and bishops, his 94 year old wife Franziska, his four daughters Hildegard, Maria, Aloisia and Rosalia, and a congregation of over 5000. In his beatification sermon, Cardinal Saraiva Martins said that Blessed Jagerstatter's witness represents "a challenge and an encouragement" for all Christians who want to "live their faith with coherence and radical commitment, even accepting extreme consequences if necessary." His courageous faith is an important example in modern times, when people face "conditioning and manipulation of consciences and minds, sometimes through deceitful means."

Conclusion

Surely, it will only be a matter of time before blessed Franz is canonised. It the meantime his witness is extremely relevant in a world where the beliefs and values of millions are so often at odds with those of Jesus Christ. In obedience to Christian conscience we need to resist all compromise with the world, the flesh and the devil. As 1 John 2:15 says, "Do not love the world... For everything in the world - the cravings of sinful flesh, the lusting of the eyes, and the boasting of what he has and does - comes not from The

Father but from the world." It is obvious from the writings of Blessed Franz that he strongly believed that those who lived according to Christian conscience, no matter what sacrifices it entailed, would enjoy eternal happiness in heaven. However, he repeatedly warned lukewarm and lapsed Catholics, who maintained, as we have seen, that "what nature demands of people cannot be sinful," were already on the train that leads to perdition. Nowadays many people have boarded, not the Nazi train, but the train of worldliness and materialism. Blessed Franz would say to them with a sense of urgency and loving concern, "Jump out before it reaches its destination, even if it costs you your life!"

Chapter Twenty Six

Fan into a Flame the Gift you have Received

This final chapter begins with a challenging verse from Romans 12:2. It reads: "Do not conform any longer to the pattern of this world, but be transformed by the renewing of your mind. Then you will be able to test and approve what God's will is, his good, pleasing and perfect will." As was mentioned already, what Paul had in mind here is the making of metal statues. The sculptor would firstly make a mould, then he would pour in the metal which would assume the pattern of the mould. Once it had hardened he would remove the completed statue from the mold. So Paul is saying, Christians are either molded by the values, attitudes and practices of the world, or by the values, attitudes and practices of Christ. In his letter he was inviting them to *metanoia*, (i.e. literally a change of mind in Greek,) so that they would move from worldly thinking to have the mind of Christ. The extent to which this transformation took place would be the extent to which they would have an experiential awareness of the guidance of the Holy Spirit. The notion of the way of the world and the way of Christ was a constant theme in the early Church. I will give just three examples.

1. The *Didache* (i.e. Teaching), which was written around 100 A.D., talks of the Christian way of life and the worldly way of death. Speaking about the latter it says in sec. 5: "The way of death is this: first of all, it is evil and completely cursed; murders, adulteries, lusts, sexual immoralities, thefts, idolatries, magic arts, sorceries, robberies, false testimonies, hypocrisies, duplicity, deceit, pride, malice, stubbornness, greed, abusive language, jealousy, audacity, arrogance, boastfulness."

2. In his homily written around 150 A.D., the author of the Second Letter of Clement, says that while the Christians talk in an inspiring manner about Christ's Way, they live in a worldly manner. He says that the pagans hear the Christian say: "It is no credit to you if you love those who love you, but it is a credit to you if you love your enemies and those who hate you," when they hear these things, they marvel at such extraordinary goodness. But when they see that not only do we not love those who hate us but do not even love those who love us, they scornfully laugh at us, and the Name is blasphemed."

3. Centuries later St. Augustine spoke about the way in which people who professed to be Catholics were so influenced by the pagan culture in which they lived that their behaviour was often indistinguishable from that of the

pagans. In one of his sermons he said to his congregation: "They give good luck presents; as for you give alms. They entertain themselves with lascivious songs; as for you, entertain yourselves with the words of scripture. They run off to the theatre, you people go to the church; they are getting drunk; you see to it that you fast. If you do all this, you have genuinely sung, Save us Lord our God, and gather us from among the nations."

Surely, the distinction between the way of the world and the way of Christ, which was mentioned in scripture and the early Christian writings, is as relevant now as it was then. All of us have been baptised and confirmed. We are Christian by name and we are called to be Christian in the way we live. However, we live in a secular culture, whose values, attitudes and beliefs often differ from those of Christianity. But if we were to look at what we do rather than what we profess, it would quickly become evident that many of us compromise with the world and its unchristian ways. I will just mention a number of the things that seem obvious to me. Many Catholics are hardly aware that they have adopted pagan, New Age beliefs such as a conviction that God is an impersonal energy, and that the world and the human race, constitutes an expression of a higher, more comprehensive divine nature. Some believe in reincarnation. They have also adopted New Age practices such as Reiki healing, getting in touch with spirit guides etc. Sadly, the rates of fornication, abortion and involvement in pornography among Catholics are often not much different from those in the rest of society. For example, I found in the U.S. that the percentage of divorces among Catholics is exactly the same as the percentage among atheists and agnostics. Without labouring the point, it is clear that there is a need for a rekindling of faith among Catholics. Let me tell you a little about what a few of us tried to do in Ireland.

Hope for the future
For quite a while I have been well aware that while we Catholics talk the talk, we don't always walk the walk. The sex abuse scandals among the clergy were a vivid and painful reminder of this sad fact. I often wondered what I and others could do about the situation. Two years ago I was heartened when I heard about an initiative being taken by three women in a Dublin prayer group. I was excited to discover that they were praying for a rekindling of faith in Ireland. To that end they aimed to collect 10,000 mass intentions which they intended to present during the celebration of a special Eucharist at the National Marian shrine in Knock. They had been inspired to do this by the example of a married couple in the 1940s. The Coynes had collected 10,000 mass intentions which were presented at Knock while praying, through Our Lady's intercession, that Ireland would be kept out of the Word War II. Happily, that prayer was answered.

I work part time for a charity called, Aid to the Church in Need. When we heard what the women were intending to do we offered them our support, which was graciously accepted. Subsequently there was an amazing response to our joint appeal for mass intentions. Within a few weeks we had received over 14,000 of them! We also printed and distributed 50,000 copies of the following prayer.

"Lord we thank you for the countless blessings you have poured out on Ireland in the past. We praise you for the way in which your grace found expression in many generous and loving lives. We are grateful for the unprecedented prosperity we currently enjoy. However, we regret, that the flame of the Spirit has sometimes been quenched by an idolatrous pursuit of power, pleasure, popularity and possessions. We confess Lord, that many of us have gone astray, and selfishly rewritten the commandments to suit ourselves. We believe that you came to cast fire on the earth and long to renew your wonders in our day as by a new Pentecost. Help us to fan the embers of our smouldering faith into a lively flame, especially by means of regular periods of personal and family prayer. Mary Mother of Jesus, we entrust Ireland to your motherly care. In the past our people remained faithful to your Son in times of persecution. We now pray that we may also remain faithful in times of prosperity. Amen."

In May 2006 we organised and participated in a pilgrimage to Knock where our Mass offerings were presented to bishop Kirby at the offertory. A DVD was made about the event, which was also reported on national T.V. and in the national press. When, afterwards, we assessed what had happened we could see that the appeal for a rekindling of faith seemed to have revealed a widespread desire among many loyal Catholics. They were not only aware of the spiritual crisis we are going through, they wanted to respond in a positive manner. It was then I began to think about ways of keeping up the momentum. How would we facilitate an ongoing renewal of faith and practice in Ireland?

I decided to write a booklet about the subject. It was inspired by a verse in 2 Timothy 1:6, "Fan into flame the gift of God, which is in you." This verse summons up the image of a coal fire which has died down and is covered with ashes. However, beneath the ashes the embers still glow with heat. If the ash is cleared away and a bellows used, the embers can be fanned into lively flames once again. It is important to note that when St. Paul encouraged Timothy to fan into a flame the gift of faith he had received, he did not tell him to ask God to do the fanning. The Lord had already poured the Holy Spirit into his heart. It was up to him to cooperate with that grace by fanning it into a flame by his own efforts. When I thought about what we could do to rekindle our faith, three things occurred to me. It could be done by means of prayer, self-denial and witness.

1) Prayer
Firstly, we need to dedicate ourselves to regular periods of personal prayer preferably with the use of scripture. However, in this chapter I want to concentrate on the importance of family prayer. In par 2685 of *The Catechism of the Catholic Church* we read: "The Christian family is the first

place of education in prayer. Based on the sacrament of marriage, the family is the "domestic church" where God's children learn to pray "as the Church" and to persevere in prayer. For young children in particular, daily family prayer is the first witness of the Church's living memory as awakened patiently by the Holy Spirit." It is not surprising therefore that Pope Paul VI asked: "Mothers, do you teach your children the Christian prayers? Do you prepare them, in conjunction with the priests and school teachers for the sacraments that they receive when they are young? Confession, Communion and Confirmation? Do you say the family Rosary together? And you, fathers, do you pray with your children...your example of honesty in thought and action, joined to some common prayer is a lesson for life, an act of worship of singular value. In this way you bring peace to your homes" (11/8/1976).

Sadly, research indicates that very few families pray together. In some cases it is due to a lack of conviction and in others due to the fact that people are so busy that families rarely spend time together e.g. at meals. They are usually distracted by such things as their own agendas, radio, T.V. etc. The booklet I referred to contains practical suggestions about how to engage in personal and family prayer. It is available from ACN Ireland, 151, St Mobhi Rd., Glasnevin, Dublin 9. Email, churchinneed@eircom.net.

2) Self-denial
St. Paul once wrote: "Everyone who competes in the games goes into strict training. They do it to get a crown that will

not last; but we do it to get a crown that will last forever. Therefore I do not run like a man running aimlessly; I do not fight like a man beating the air. No, I beat my body and make it my slave so that after I have preached to others, I myself will not be disqualified for the prize", 1 Cor 9:24-27.

In modern Christianity, spiritual exercises are sometimes referred to as ascetical practices. The words 'ascetic' and 'asceticism' are derived from the Greek meaning 'to exercise.' Christians realise that just as working-out is vital for success in modern sports, especially professional ones, so it is equally vital in spirituality. Good intentions are not enough. Self-indulgent, lazy tendencies need to be overcome if people are to carry out the great command of loving others in the way that Jesus has loved us. In this regard I have two practical suggestions to make.

Firstly, we know that the members of the New Testament Church fasted regularly. It served a number of purposes, to make satisfaction for sin; control bodily passions; experience solidarity with the poor; and express, in a symbolic way, a creaturely dependence on God. Fasting can take a number of forms:

1. Abstaining for a while from activities which might be harmful, such as smoking, eating junk food, watching too much T.V. etc.
2. A partial fast, such as eating one or two meals less, or taking no nourishment except liquids e.g. juices, milk, soup and the like.
3. A normal fast where the person only drinks water.

There is reliable evidence that indicates that fasting purifies the heart, strengthens self-discipline and prepares the soul to receive inspirations from God.

Secondly, we need to be generous in giving money to the poor and oppressed in Ireland, Britain and abroad. Listen to what God says in Deuteronomy 15:11-12: "Give liberally and be ungrudging when you do so, for on this account the Lord your God will bless you in all your work and in all that you undertake. Since there will never cease to be some in need on the earth, I therefore command you, "Open your hand to the poor and needy neighbour in your land."

3) Witness

We Catholics need to courageously witness to our faith instead of being afraid to talk about it because of fear of ridicule or criticism. Here is a story, borrowed from Alpha, which illustrates what I mean. A young cadet was taking his final exam in the police academy. Here is the situation he was asked about.

"You are on patrol in the city centre when a gas main explodes in a nearby street. On investigation you find that a large hole has been blown in the footpath. There is an overturned van lying nearby. Inside the van there is a strong smell of alcohol. Both occupants – a man and a woman – are injured. You recognise the woman as the wife of the police chief who is out of the country at an international police conference. A passing motorist stops to offer assistance and you realise that he is a man who is wanted for armed robbery. Suddenly a man runs out of a nearby house, shouting that the explosion has caused his wife to go into labour and that she needs help. Another man is crying for help, having been blown into the river. He cannot swim and needs to be rescued. In a few words, what action would you take? The young police cadet thought for a moment and wrote, "I'd take off my uniform and mingle with the crowd!"

Many Catholics are comfortable being Christian in the presence of other practicing Christians, but feel like taking off the uniform of Christian belief and values in secular company. This is the problem we spoke about at the beginning of the chapter; the fact that we don't always practice what we profess.

As was noted in chapter twenty three, we can witness to our faith in small but effective verbal and non verbal ways. For instance if someone asks, "were you at the game on Sunday," you could say, "yes I went after attending mass." When dining out you can make the sign of the cross before saying the grace, and refrain from taking the holy name of Jesus in vain. Another way of witnessing to our faith is by standing up for our Christian values when controversial issues are being discussed at work, in a restaurant, or wherever. When it seems appropriate we can also tell part of our own faith story. St. Peter gave sage advice when he said: "Always be prepared to give an answer to everyone who asks you to give the reason for the hope you have. But do this with gentleness and respect", 1 Pt 3:15.

Conclusion

The members of the Charismatic Renewal in these islands are in debt to Margaret Thomas and her fellow pilgrims. In response to a word of prophecy given at the Newman Consultation in 2005, they went on pilgrimage to Assisi. During that time of prayerful obedience to what they believed was God's word, they felt that "the whole of the pilgrimage was saying, re-build my church. This is a call to the individuals involved but we suggest also to all of the Catholic Charismatic Renewal...This requires unity both in ecumenical and internationally....We are not to expect a renewal of the renewal or a new outpouring of the Holy Spirit but are to keep opening the great gifts that were given in 1967...We pray that we may all be set free from any discouragement at the current state of Christianity in our lands" Goodnews (March/April 2008), pp. 10-11. How true. We can respond by re-kindling our faith as a result of taking the three practical steps briefly referred to here.

Further copies of this book
and all Fr. Pat's books
are available from

Goodnews Books & Resources
St. John the Apostle Church Buildings
296 Sundon Park Road
Luton, Beds. LU3 3AL

+44 01582 571011
www.goodnewsbooks.net
orders@goodnewsbooks.net